Decision Making and
Administration in Higher Education

Decision Making
and Administration
in Higher Education

JOHN D. MILLETT

The Kent State University Press

Second Printing
Copyright © 1968 by John D. Millett
All rights reserved
Manufactured in the United States of America
Designed by Merald E. Wrolstad
First Edition

Library of Congress Card Catalogue Number 68-55383
Standard Book Number 87338-030-4

TO MY COLLEAGUES
OF
MIAMI UNIVERSITY
IN
WARM REMEMBRANCE
OF
SHARED EXPERIENCE

Preface

The essays which comprise this little volume were initially prepared for various higher education conferences. Three of these in particular are mentioned in connection with the individual chapters herein. One of the papers was originally prepared for a seminar session of interns in academic administration conducted in 1966 by the Center for Research and Development in Higher Education of the University of California, Berkeley, on behalf of the American Council on Education. An abbreviated version of this paper was published in *College and University Business,* volume 44 (February, 1968).

It is inevitable when papers are written for different groups at different times for the author to repeat certain ideas and to express certain beliefs in several different ways. I have not endeavored to eliminate these apparent repetitions. I believe my major concern with program budgeting in higher education, with new organizational arrangements involving faculty and students in the decision-making process, and with the financial needs of higher education deserves the emphasis of repetition.

These essays have been based upon my nearly twenty years of experience with higher educational administration: for four years in the study of financial problems, for eleven years as a state university president, and now in my fifth year as chief executive officer for a state-wide board of higher education. Necessarily, the problems and the observations discussed here are drawn from that experience. No doubt others with a different background and with different attitudes would offer different observations. I suggest only that these particular points of view presented here represent concerns which are anything but peculiar to a single individual and identify problems which must necessarily be of urgent interest to many persons.

I am grateful to several individuals for comments and suggestions about these essays and to my administrative associates who have assisted me in their preparation.

John D. Millett

Columbus, Ohio
July 1, 1968

Contents

New Patterns
of Decision Making

The colleges and universities in the United States are experiencing a dual revolution in our day. Internally, a new pattern of decision-making procedure is emerging. Externally, more and more authority affecting the activities and operations of colleges and universities is being exercised by agencies of government. The full extent and impact of these changes are at best but dimly perceived at the present time.

It is well to remember that the American college or university was never quite so autonomous in the control of its affairs as some romanticists would have us believe. The church-related college or university has always had its parent religious denomination to consider. No privately sponsored college or university could ever afford to be indifferent to its actual or potential benefactors.

A shortened version of this paper was presented at the 23rd Annual National Conference on Higher Education of the American Association for Higher Education in Chicago on March 4, 1968.

1

Publicly sponsored colleges or universities have always had to concern themselves with the real or probable reaction of chief executives and legislatures. Voluntary associations, including accrediting bodies and the American Association of University Professors, have had substantial influence upon the programs, the curricula, and the costs of higher education. By their studies and their gifts, private foundations have had a considerable impact upon the academic practices of colleges and universities. The individual college or university in America has never been so isolated or so independent as some persons have suggested.

It is conventional wisdom in the field of higher education always to declare that each college and each university in the United States is different. Within certain limits, this declaration has some factual validity. Yet few colleges and universities have ever been able, or eager, to avoid the "mainstream" of academic development in this country. While institutions have had their own unique attributes of identity, their own particular sense of mission and dedication, their own history of leadership (good, bad, and indifferent), their own separate traditions, and their own individual record of financial support, these institutions have had their similarities of experience as well.

In general, the pattern of decision-making in most American colleges and universities from the time of the Civil War until World War II was not too different, one from another. The prevailing pattern of authority emphasized the special role of the president. To be sure, legally, the authority to make final decisions about matters of educational policy, financial management, appointments and other personnel actions, and physical facilities was vested in the board of trustees. Undoubtedly, the presidential point of view was influenced by the known attitudes of important board members, especially board members who enjoyed considerable economic or political power. It is unfortunate that we have so little information about the decision-making pattern which has arisen between board members and college or university presidents. In my own personal experience, the presidents I have had an opporunity to observe have had dominant personalities. In most instances these presidents were likely to be supported in their actions by their boards. In some cases which I have heard about but not observed, presidents have been almost errand boys for two or three powerful board members.

In any event, faculty members for the most part in these years had only modest influence upon the operations of colleges or universities as institutions. These faculty members in a good many colleges and universities enjoyed, to a considerable extent, personal or group discretion in academic matters. They usually determined course requirements for a degree, the curricular program, course content and teaching procedure, and the evaluation of student performance. The faculty also usually had a major voice in establishing the desired standards of student social behavior. Faculty members came into conflict with presidents and boards of trustees when some individual faculty member became active in political or social controversy outside the classroom. Only gradually, as the concept of academic freedom developed, did some standards of conduct and procedure in these instances emerge.[1]

In this period before World War II, students were generally expected to abide by the rules of conduct imposed by their elders. Many campuses experienced at some time one or more student "rebellions," and students then as now exercised a good deal of individual ingenuity in finding ways to circumvent restrictions upon their social behavior, whether or not these had to do with drinking, card-playing, dancing, closing hours, or "improper" conduct. Most students were undergraduate students, the college took seriously its role of parental supervision, and the church influence on college attitudes (whether the college was privately or publicly sponsored) was strong. Ideas about student government were limited, student publications were bothersome but carefully scrutinized, and student social organizations were mostly individualistic in orientation. Student "power" was impossible to imagine under these circumstances.

It is possible to offer many explanations for these cir-

---

1. Cf. especially Robert M. MacIver, *Academic Freedom in Our Time* (New York: Columbia University Press, 1955); and Richard Hofstadter and Walter P. Metzger, *The Development of Academic Freedom in the United States* (New York: Columbia University Press, 1955).

cumstances as they existed before 1940. Colleges and universities attempted at best a modest role in American society. The church influence remained active and the social and economic status of faculty members except in a handful of institutions was quite similar to that of the clergy. Colleges and universities were relatively small, and only a small proportion of the college age population was enrolled. The American culture was fairly simple in technology, in economic operations, in intellectual endeavor. Indeed, the politics of the era have been labeled the politics of "deference," and the designation might be applied to higher education as well.

Whether this sketch is accurate or not, few will deny that at least it certainly does not describe the American college or university of the past thirty years. There may be those who regard the past with nostalgic longing, but that this past has disappeared as irrevocably in pattern as it has in time can scarcely be argued.

THE ROLE OF THE FACULTY

The prevailing expectation today is that the collective faculty in a college or university will enjoy "shared authority" with the administration in decision-making about the institution. The problem of our day is to define what is meant by shared authority and to give that definition concrete meaning in the everyday, continuing operation of a college or university.

A recent report by a task force set up by the American

Association for Higher Education describes "five zones" in the distribution of decision-making authority between faculty and administration.[2] These were labeled (1) administrative dominance, (2) administrative primacy, (3) shared authority, (4) faculty primacy, and (5) faculty dominance. The task force reported that in a sampling of thirty-four colleges and universities it found that about one-half were characterized by administrative primacy, one-quarter by shared authority, and the remaining one-quarter were characterized by administrative dominance, although a few fell in the category of faculty primacy. The sample was admittedly not constructed on a representative basis; it included twenty-eight public and six private institutions. The twenty-eight public institutions included only two well-established state universities; the others were twelve community colleges, seven state colleges, and seven new state universities.

In describing the characteristics of the five patterns of decision-making, the AAHE report provided only broad outlines of administrative practice. Administrative dominance was described as an arrangement in which the administration made decisions on a unilateral basis, with little or no prior faculty consultation. Administrative primacy was apparently an arrangement where there were mechanisms for faculty consultation or expression of point of view but these opinions were given less con-

2. *Faculty Participation in Academic Governance* (Washington: American Association for Higher Education, 1967).

sideration than administrative recommendations. Although the report does not indicate who gave the "less consideration," presumably the reference is to boards of trustees. Shared authority is described as a pattern in which both faculty and administration exercise effective influence in decision-making. From the account it appears that shared authority exists when educational policy is determined by a faculty senate and when there is some joint machinery between administration and faculty for resolving personnel issues. Faculty primacy means that decision-making authority rests primarily with the faculty, and faculty dominance means that all basic authority resides with the faculty.

Before making certain comments about this effort to categorize decision-making authority, we should note two "findings" set forth by the AAHE report. The task force declared that faculty unrest was primarily evident in public junior colleges and in the new or "emerging" public four-year colleges and universities. The group also reported that much faculty unrest was centered in the increasing extent of decision-making authority vested in agencies beyond the campus itself. Unfortunately, the AAHE report did not consider either of these "facts" in any detail. For example, it might be suggested that junior colleges which were created as a projection of local high schools and that state teachers colleges controlled by state boards of education tended to have administrative arrangements patterned after public school systems rather than the older "established" public universities. It might also be suggested that an increasing expectation of government funds to support higher education must necessarily involve the development of a government bureaucracy handling the administration of such funds.

There are two observations which need to be made before we look in more detail at the whole subject of the faculty role in college or university decision-making. Almost all such discussions begin with the proposition that "the administration" and "the faculty" constitute disparate, antithetical, and mutually hostile groups in the academic community. The other observation is a simple fact. Every organized enterprise must have a system of management, an administrative apparatus. A college or a university cannot exist without a structure and process of administration. It is unfortunate that discussions of the phenomenon of power in an academic community —and that is what a pattern of decision-making authority is—do not begin with a careful, explicit statement of assumptions.

It is unfortunate to begin a discussion of college or university decision-making on the assumption that administration and faculty do constitute antithetical forces within the academic community. I recognize that there is a good deal of historical experience in which boards of trustees and presidents have appeared as exercising authority without concern for faculty attitudes or recommendations. I know that some university presidents have lacked prior experience in higher education and that some presidents, both with and without experience as a faculty member, have displayed evidence of authoritarian behavior in their actions. These circumstances are unfortunate, but my guess is that any such tendencies as these are disappearing rather than increasing in American higher education.

If we were to develop a pattern of faculty dominance in the decision-making authority in higher education, this would not suddenly eliminate all administration from the operation of a college or university. There would still be financial resources to collect and augment, budgets to adopt and execute, accounting records to maintain, supplies to be purchased and stored, buildings to plan and maintain, non-academic employees to be hired and retained, facilities to be utilized and controlled, housing to be provided students, and services to be operated (such as water, heat, light, sewerage, and communication). This enumeration says nothing about the direction of the educational operation itself, including instruction, research, and public service.

Let us return to the proposition that what colleges and universities are seeking today is a pattern of shared authority in decision-making. I believe we may assume that the legal authority for governance of colleges and universities will continue to be vested in a board of trustees, self-perpetuating in the case of privately sponsored institutions and appointed by public authority or even elected by the voters in the case of publicly sponsored institutions. I think we may also assume that presidents will continue formally to be appointed by boards of trustees. The internal problem then is to find a meaningful and useful structure of providing recommendations for action to this board of trustees.

In 1966 the American Association of University Professors, the American Council on Education, and the Association of Governing Boards of Universities and Colleges issued a joint "Statement on Government of Colleges and Universities." This statement began with a declaration that the tasks of institutions of higher education produced an "inescapable interdependence" among governing boards, administrators, faculty, students, and others. The statement then called for "joint planning and effort" on the part of the constituent groups of an academic community.

The joint statement of 1966 emphasized the importance of determining the general educational policy of an institution: the size and composition of the student body, the standards of admission and of performance expected of students, and the "relative emphasis" to be given to instruction and research in the program of the institution. These were matters requiring participation in decision-making by governing board, administration, and faculty. The statement suggested that within the board framework of such general educational policies it was the "primary" responsibility of the faculty to determine the appropriate curriculum and procedures of instruction.

The joint statement of 1966 called for joint effort, involving the "broadest possible exchange of information and opinion," in planning, in determining requirements and priorities for physical facilities, and in budgeting. The statement called for "cooperation" between board and faculty in the selection of a president and consultation in the selection of academic deans and other academic officers, but indicated that determinations involving faculty status would "ordinarily" be determined by faculty groups. The statement cautioned that only the board as a board could speak "legally" for the whole institution, although it might delegate this assignment to an agent.

The 1966 joint statement went on to outline the respective roles of governing boards, president, and faculty in college or university government. The governing board is expected to help relate the institution to its community. In exercising its final authority in matters of educational policy, operation, and management, the board is expected to be guided by the judgment of administrative staff and faculty. The board is expected to help defend the vested interests of society in the educational institution. The president's role is primarily that of institutional leadership. The president seeks to ensure that standards and procedures of the institution conform to stated policy and "sound academic practice." The president seeks to conserve and augment the resources available to the institution. The faculty is concerned with curriculum, degree requirements, instructional procedure, research activity, faculty status, student academic performance, and the utilization of instructional resources.

The difficulty with this kind of prescription of the respective roles of governing board, administrative staff, and faculty is that it acknowledges a shared interest without providing a clear-cut structure of authority. Suppose a governing board and a faculty speaking by majority vote have different judgments about desirable college or university policy or practice. Legally, it is simple to say that the judgment of the governing board is final. But the faculty may not acquiesce in this decision. The consequence is then continued strife within the academic community.

The president's position between governing board and faculty is crucial in the decision-making process. The critical factor is the president's capacities as an academic leader. It is clear that faculties in colleges and universities are determined to have a substantial voice in the decision-making process. The difficulty with this situation is that faculties as collective bodies of individuals have not faced up to the problem of leadership, either the problem of mechanisms for selecting a leader or the problem of defining the leadership role. Under these circumstances, the president has the opportuinty for academic leadership. The issue remains whether the president has the capacity for effective leadership within the academic community.

Discussions of desirable structure for faculty participation in college or university governance usually begin with a description of a department and department chairman. Beyond the department is the faculty of a college or other general instructional body within a university. Beyond the college is the university as a whole, where prevailing practice now prescribes a faculty council or faculty senate elected on a representative basis. Departments, college faculties, and faculty councils serve a dual purpose. They usually enjoy certain decision-making authority in matters of personnel and certain other academic matters. This authority may be prescribed by college or university regulations or ordinances or may be the result of customary usage. In addition, these same bodies may debate and recommend action on any matter of concern to the academic community. The problem of academic organization and operation is whether these debates and recommendations constitute decisions or simply proposals. A president may present such recommendations to the governing board. On some occasions the president may recommend a different course of action, and on other occasions a board may not agree with president and faculty.

There are two major deficiencies in faculty decision-making which affect the degree of "finality" which may be accorded their proposals for institutional action. One deficiency is the possible inadequate attention given to the administrative feasibility of the proposed course of action. Obviously, the availability of financial resources is a continuing restraint upon academic decision-making. A college or university can only spend as much as it receives in income, and the pattern of expenditures must ensure preservation of the institution. Otherwise, the liquidation of the college or university becomes the policy objective. But every decision is usually a matter of administration and of cost. Policy decisions are expressions of pious platitudes unless carried out, and administration of action requires resources. Unless a faculty is intimately aware of the administrative capabilities and costs involved in every decision, faculty decision-making is likely to be administratively and financially irresponsible. Under such circumstances, a governing board may necessarily feel compelled to overrule faculty decisions.

In the second place, a faculty may be insensitive to public reactions which affect the institution's access to enlarge financial resources and general public standing. It seems probable that more disagreements and friction between faculties and governing boards and presidents arise because of this difference in outlook than from any other cause. Indeed, the most important characteristic of faculties in most colleges and universities today is their ambivalence toward the world outside the college or university itself. Many faculty members perceive their role primarily in terms of criticizing the conventional wisdom of society. And indeed this is a major function of faculty members. But often this criticism is presented in ways designed to shock many persons and groups in society, and sometimes the criticism is presented with a dogma and authoritarianism which ill-accords with the scholarly traditions of cautious acceptance of any concept of knowledge. On the other hand, faculties are dependent upon this external society for that affluence which faculty members have now achieved and for the affluence to which they aspire.

Apart from student charges, the financing of higher education depends upon the philanthropy of persons (including corporations and private foundations) and the grants of governments. The availability of both depends upon individual and collective reactions of power persons in society ourside the walls of a college or university. The president finds his most trying challenges when on the one hand he is supposed to "bring home the bacon" and on the other hand is asked to defend faculty members who belittle the intelligence and behavior of those who raise pigs. This is the heart of all problems in faculty-administrative relationships in American higher education today.

COLLECTIVE BARGAINING

Here I can do no more than call attention to still another recent factor in the pattern of college or university decision-making—the factor of unionization and collective bargaining.[3] There is some effort being made at the present time in some colleges and universities to move away from the concept of "shared authority" or of "joint effort" between governing board and faculty to a concept of management and labor. Under this new concept a faculty

3. Cf. Harry A. Marmion, "Unions and Higher Education," *Educational Record,* vol. 49 (winter, 1968), p. 41.

would organize itself as a labor union, would enter into a process of collective bargaining with the governing board, and would perform its work for the college or university in accordance with a contract of agreement.

There are many unanswered questions about the whole concept of management-faculty bargaining and agreement as a pattern of decision-making for colleges and universities. To what extent is the analogy of management-labor relations in private business applicable to the academic community? To what extent is the professional status of faculty members compatible with union status? How will union membership of faculty members affect the faculty membership in scholarly associations? How will collective bargaining agreements affect the determination of the educational objectives and programs of a college or university? How will collective bargaining agreements affect the instructional process? How is it proposed to obtain the income for a college or university needed to carry out collective bargaining agreements? And is it intended that collective bargaining agreements shall be made college by college, university by university, or upon an "industry-wide" basis?

These are important questions, and they deserve careful consideration. These questions cannot receive the attention here they deserve. Yet one general observation may be useful. There is some uncertainty about the *real* party which unionization of faculty seeks to involve in the consideration of faculty goals. To some faculty members, no doubt the president and governing board appear as hostile elements in the college or university, and collective bargaining seems to be a new, perhaps more effective method for making faculty decision-making meaningful in the academic community. In other instances, faculties may regard collective bargaining and the threat of a strike as an effective method of exerting pressure upon the general public to provide greater resources for college and university operations. Higher education has never organized and has never exerted pressure in the political process in the same way that public schools have utilized parent-teacher bodies and educational associations. Some faculty members may believe that collective bargaining and strike action are their best available means for obtaining their desired share of the economic resources of society.

It seems likely that the collective bargaining process must introduce some far-reaching changes in the determination of educational objectives and instructional procedures. It would seem likely that these aspects of college or university operation would fall in large part upon the administrative staff, including deans. It may even be necessary to look upon department chairmen as supervisors and foremen, not as union members. Under this arrangement, collective bargaining agreements would have to spell out the instructional role of faculties and every faculty member would be expected to fulfill the obligations of the bargaining contract. It is less clear how research and public service activities would be performed by faculty members under collective bargaining contracts. It is perhaps no accident that the institutions where collective bargaining has been seriously considered have usually been institutions where instruction was the preponderant activity and research was a minor endeavor.

STUDENT POWER

An additional factor in the current decision-making process of colleges and universities is student power. Although a concern with student conduct has characterized American colleges since they were first established, and although the welfare of students has been a continuing preoccupation of higher education in this country, only recently has the student body come to be regarded as a constituent element of the academic community with a role to play in the determination of educational policies and practices.

It is essential to draw a sharp distinction between college or university activity designed to promote and regulate student social behavior and activity designed to establish standards of academic behavior. Unfortunately, problems of social conduct and problems of academic conduct are frequently confused with each other. Even if we grant that the two are inter-related, I believe it is possible to draw a distinction between social conduct and academic conduct. I would even go a step farther and argue that in the past many colleges and universities have given primary attention in their relations to students with problems of social conduct. Today, it is evident that the primary concern must and should be problems of academic conduct.

Because colleges and universities developed in an America which was preponderantly rural in its economy and its distribution of population, the college in a small town became a prevailing geographical arrangement. Only a few colleges were established in large cities. The college in a small town had to provide a home as well as an education for its students. "Going away to college" became a social practice and a social tradition. Thus, the college found itself confronted with the necessity of providing residence halls for students, together with eating facilities. Soon there were problems of social organization (literary societies, eating clubs, fraternities), student activities (newspapers, yearbooks, academic clubs, athletics, dances and social affairs), student recreation (sports, games), and student health to worry about. Then there were problems of social conduct to handle: drinking, gambling, fighting (dueling), stealing, destruction of property, relations with the other sex. Most colleges and universities developed rather stringent codes of conduct for student social behavior consistent with the prevailing standards of a society with a puritan tradition and a strong sense of family responsibility.

Today colleges and universities have found that their codes of conduct which they seek to enforce no longer fit the prevailing practice of society at large, or that their codes of conduct no longer fit a highly urbanized environment. In addition, students insist that they should participate in both the determination of codes of conduct and their enforcement. The result is that more and more attention is being given to modification of standards of social conduct. In some instances, the very question is raised whether social conduct should be the concern of a college or university.

To the extent that students live in an academic community—not just attend it—some standards of social conduct appear to be essential. Otherwise, social activity and behavior may well border on anarchy. Furthermore, there are colleges and universities which conceive of social activity as a reinforcement of the educational process and therefore seek to provide such standards as are essential to the integration of social behavior and the learning process. In some instances, students may move from a protective home environment into a non-authoritarian academic environment and find the social freedom so heady as to interfere with academic performance. On occasion, even today colleges find themselves in the role of having to provide an education in social responsibility as well as in academic achievement.

In 1967 a committee established by five organizations (the Association of American Colleges, the American Association of University Professors, the National Student Association, the National Association of Student Personnel Administrators, and the National Association of Women Deans and Counselors) prepared and published a "Joint Statement on Rights and Freedoms of Students."[4]

4. The text was published in *The Chronicle of Higher Education*, August 23, 1967.

This statement was intended to set forth certain guidelines for action at individual colleges and universities. The statement was divided into five parts: freedom of access (admission), in the classroom, student records, student affairs, off-campus freedom, and discipline. Only two or three parts of the statement need specific mention here.

The joint 1967 statement declares: "The student body should have clearly defined means to participate in the formulation and application of institutional policy affecting academic and student affairs." There is no indication, however, how this participation should be structured or how much weight is to be given to student viewpoints in the determination of academic and student policies. The statement does give considerable attention to freedom of association and freedom of press for students.

On the matter of off-campus freedom, the 1967 joint statement emphasizes that students are citizens and urges that off-campus behavior should be subject to state and local law, not institutional regulation. There is no indication exactly how to define off-campus behavior in contrast with on-campus behavior, and no suggestion about standards of desirable conduct by students on campus in support of groups and causes with an off-campus focus.

On the subject of discipline, the 1967 statement is emphatic in asserting that educational institutions "have a duty and the corollary disciplinary powers to protect their educational purpose through the setting of standards of scholarship and conduct for students who attend them and through the regulation of the use of institutional facilities." The statement goes on to assert: "The institution has an obligation to clarify those standards of behavior which it considers essential to its educational mission and its community life." The statement then emphasizes the importance of "procedural fairness" in the administration of discipline.

The interest of students in the institution of higher education they attend can be an asset of great importance. It is unfortunate that the issues which arise are so often issues only indirectly related to the educational mission of the institution. It must be recognized, also, that student groups may be encouraged by groups off-campus to involve themselves and the institution they attend in social controversies in the general community as distinct from the academic community. Here the purpose may be to utilize the prestige of higher education in other causes. Or the objective may be to disrupt or even destroy the service which higher education renders society.

Perhaps the least understood and the least considered issue involving the very essence of the educational process and the integrity of higher education institutions is that of the relationship between education and society. The student activists of the 1960's deserve credit for their action in bringing this issue to the fore. It is unfortunate that the academic staff of higher education in general has done little to clarify or illuminate this issue. And student activists for the most part have taken a position without careful consideration of its implications or consequences.

In the long run, the phenomenon of student power has one basic implication. Shall students determine the educational objectives and the procedures of institutions of higher education, or shall these objectives be determined by trustees and professional educators on behalf of society? It is one thing to say that students should participate in college or university decision-making. It is another thing to say that students should decide what they want to learn and how they want to learn it. There have been occasions when some students recently have seemed to be saying that students should determine what they want to learn and should consult faculty members about this learning, only when the students desire to do so. Such an attitude implies the assumption that learning serves a student society only and not any larger society. Such an attitude implies a permanent alienation of students from society, or the substitution of a student society for existing society. These implications are revolutionary. They may also be nihilistic. When will students learn that it is easier to criticize than to change, easier to destroy than to build, easier to disengage than to participate constructively and effectively? It is this kind of learning which society needs, and which maturity promoted by the learning process should evidence.

FEDERAL GOVERNMENT

At the same time when colleges and universities are experiencing substantial change in the decision-making process internally, more and more decisions affecting the policies and practices of these institutions are being made externally. Although the President of the United States on one occasion described the role of the federal government as that of "junior partner" in the higher education enterprise, American universities are almost completely dependent upon the federal government for support of research projects.

Since 1958 the federal government has also been a major source of funds in support of student aid activity by colleges and universities. The National Defense Education Act of 1958 provided for a system of low-interest student loans to assist students in meeting the expense of higher education and also established a limited program of graduate fellowship funds to be given to universities. The federal government has assumed an important role in financing continuing education projects, especially institutes and seminars to upgrade science and other education at the elementary and secondary level and to improve management or other skills in the public service.

More recently, as the result of legislation in 1963 and in 1965, the federal government has begun to make matching grants for the construction of academic facilities, for the purchase of instructional equipment, for improvements in teacher education, and for improvements in so-called "developing" institutions. The federal government has made funds available to assist the construction of medical school facilities and facilities for allied health professions. The student aid program has been extended through educational opportunity grants for students from low-income families and through work-study grants.

In general, it should be noted that as of 1968 the federal government, with certain negligible exceptions, did not provide any funds in support of the instructional function of colleges and universities. It should also be noted that the federal government tended to make its grants and loans equally available to institutions with private sponsorship as to institutions with public sponsorship.

In connection with our primary concern here, there are two major issues which should be noted insofar as federal government support of higher education is concerned. One of these issues is that of the selection of the institutions to receive federal financial assistance. The second issue is whether the federal government should utilize the mechanism of loans and grants for categorical purposes as a means of influencing general educational policies. Both issues raise questions of great importance to the decision-making process.

In the administration of research grants, the federal granting agencies early took the position that grants should be made to individuals presenting projects which were inherently promising and to individuals having an established research reputation. The objective was to strengthen the research capabilities and opportunities available to known scholars. As a consequence, it was soon found that research grants tended to go to a few outstanding universities which had brought together or retained notable groups of scholars. The best supported universities from private sources and state sources became the best supported centers of research activity by the federal government. The complaint arose that the rich became richer and the poor were condemned to continuing poverty. Moreover, federal research support was concentrated in the fields of the physical sciences, engineering, the biological sciences, medicine, and mathematics.

The alternative to selection of institutions and scholars according to some criterion of excellence, however subjective or objective this criterion may be, was selection on a population basis. Selection might also be based upon promise of future development, or upon some scale of need. All of these additional criteria have been employed in various federal programs of financial assistance to higher education.

The inevitable fact in any selection system other than a straight apportionment of available funds according to state population or institutional enrollment is that federal granting agencies must evaluate institutional status. If a college or university wants federal funds, it must be able to meet the standards fixed by federal agencies as the minimum qualification for federal financial assistance. Thus, colleges and universities are no longer autonomous but become supplicants for funds and must modify their behavior accordingly.

In addition, once the federal government became a large-scale supplier of financial resources, it was of course possible to utilize these funds to achieve various objectives deemed desirable by federal legislators and federal administrators. Federal grants became available, accordingly, only to educational institutions which pledged to make their facilities and programs available without regard to race, religion, or national origin. Federal construction grants became available only if institutions let contracts by competitive bidding and observed all federal minimum wage rates and minimum working conditions. Then federal construction grants were made available only if contractors provided equal opportunity in the recruitment of labor, regardless of union contracts. It was suggested also in 1968 that grants should go to colleges and universities only if they were engaged in programs to help the poverty groups in large cities.

Federal funds do mean various kinds of control and do exercise various kinds of influence upon the decision-making of colleges and universities. Of course, any institution may refuse federal grants or loans. But when institutions are seeking increased funds and are hard-pressed financially, they cannot be both affluent and autonomous.

STATE GOVERNMENTS

At the level of state government, two different but inter-related organizational changes have been occurring in the past twenty years. One of these is the development of the multi-campus college or university system. The other is the appearance of the state-wide coordinating board.

It may be well to point out here that there are twelve states in the United States with a single, state-wide governing board of public higher education. Among other states, such state-wide governing boards exist in Georgia, Florida, Mississippi, Iowa, Kansas, Arizona, and Oregon. In some of these instances, the junior colleges function under separate agencies of administrative direction and supervision. The public colleges and universities in these twelve states have for a long time been accustomed to centralized board direction. Actually, we know very little about how these state-wide governing boards have performed their work. It is possible that such boards in practice have tended to consider the problems of each institution separately. It is also possible that they have acted as a state-wide planning and policy agency.

In the years after World War II, many state universities expanded their enrollment capacity by establishing new campuses. The University of California had pioneered this kind of action as early as the 1920's with the establishment of a "branch" in Los Angeles, a branch which now has practically all of the dimensions of the original campus in Berkeley. Sometimes state universities created two-year campuses. In some instances, as state teachers colleges became multi-purpose institutions, new central boards of trustees took over the direction of these colleges from state boards of education. The most unusual multi-campus public university today is, of course, the State University of New York.

The multi-campus state college or state university system has had to find the administrative procedures appropriate to a geographically dispersed operation. Some administrative officers seemed to think that the administrative process appropriate to a single campus could be applied to a multi-campus organization. The centralization of decision-making which resulted has caused apoplexy. Little by little, boards and administrators of multi-campus operations have been learning how to decentralize the administrative process.

The state-wide coordinating board which now exists in some twenty-two states has had a different problem. This board has confronted a highly decentralized administrative process and has had to decide to what extent certain common concerns of all state institutions should be brought together for central decision-making.

It is not easy to determine just what are the appropriate subjects for centralized and decentralized decision-making. Necessarily, any one pattern may not fit all situations and all changing circumstances. But in general certain common guidelines do seem possible.

First of all, if a state is to have a master plan for

higher education development, it seems clear that this will have to be prepared and decided by a central agency. To be sure, individual institutions and groups may and should be invited to contribute suggestions and criticisms of a master plan. But when the decision is made, it will have to be that of a central agency. One may debate the merits of the master plan concept, but if it is desired to have a master plan for the state or for the federal government, it is going to be provided at the level of the central decision-making authority.

Insofar as governmental budgeting is concerned, it is equally obvious that these decisions will have to be made by the chief executive and the legislature, utilizing such central sources of advice as a budget office or a coordinating board as the governmental officials may choose. Institutions of higher education may request funds and may seek to obtain income from diversified sources, but the final decisions about the allocation of funds are going to be made where these funds arise.

A difficult question in the financing of higher education is the extent to which purposes shall be specified and the expenditure of funds shall be controlled when they are provided from a central source. I submit that state government agencies tend to confer greater autonomy upon individual colleges and universities than do federal government agencies in this respect.

There are a host of other issues which may be resolved on a centralized or decentralized basis. These include admission policies and procedures, the location of new campuses, limitations of enrollment size at particular campuses, articulation of student movement among campuses, the introduction of new instructional programs, and the assignment of missions and roles to various institutions. If these decisions are to be made on a centralized basis, they ought to be made, I believe, in accordance with a master plan.

There are several vital aspects of higher education which remain largely under the jurisdiction of the individual campus. These include requirements for a degree, curriculum construction, instructional methods, student conduct regulation, internal organizational structure, the solicitation of funds from private sources and even from federal agencies, and the careful management of available resources to obtain maximum output. The criticism of outside interference is sometimes, I believe, a smoke screen to conceal failures or inefficiencies in internal management.

No pattern of decision-making authority between central agencies and local campuses can ever be effective without mutual understanding and concern, common respect, and a shared devotion to the great ends of higher education.

The Planning Process
in American Higher Education

It is very difficult to discuss the concept of planning in an enterprise without resort to a number of time-honored cliches. Planning is a major technique of direction in any organized endeavor. Planning is a process for anticipating future conditions and preparing to meet them. Planning fixes objectives and seeks the efficient utilization of resources in the realization of desired outputs. Planning is a continuous activity which constantly seeks to meet changing circumstances, changing needs, and changing ideas. Planning produces plans; the plans must be judged in terms of the results they project and achieve. Planning is a duty of management, an essential ingredient in decision-making. Planning needs the participation of all groups or elements in a structured operation. Planning depends upon knowledge but cannot wait for research to produce new knowledge upon the basis of which more effective

An Address for the Administrative Improvement Seminar, Saint Joseph's College Rensselaer, Indiana February 15, 1968 plans might be prepared. Planning is preparation for action.

Behind these oft-mentioned characteristics of the planning process are some very important admonitions. It is surprising when one examines a particular planning process in some specific enterprise how frequently one finds that these elementary aspects of planning have been ignored.

At the end of World War II, I wrote a book about the process and organization of government planning. In it I made a distinction between *policy* planning and *program* planning. This distinction, more than twenty years later, is still of major importance. The planning effort or activity of an enterprise must encompass both policies *and* programs.

Policy planning can be differentiated from program planning in several respects. For one thing, policy planning gives special attention to the more intangible concerns of an enterprise, to the basic value judgments upon which an enterprise predicates its whole endeavor. For another thing, policy planning entails long-range objectives, the primary goals which an enterprise dedicates its efforts to achieving. Program planning, on the other hand, seeks to find the ways and means whereby policy objectives can be realized. Obviously, both policy planning and program planning are closely inter-related. We may postulate some noble and far-reaching goals for our organized activities, but the means of achieving them may not be available. It is more realistic and less frustrating under some circumstances for men to modify their policy objectives. There is also the danger that we may let our judgment about the deficiency of program means betray us into abandoning great purposes which deserve our most devoted effort. Dream no little dreams, an early urban planner said, for they lack the power to inspire men's souls.

Let me illustrate my definition of policy planning by use of an example from higher education. Any planner in higher education must begin by asking: shall higher education seek to provide opportunity for every high school graduate or only a selected proportion of the high school graduates? The answer to this question depends upon a definition of the objectives of higher education and upon a formulation of programs which are appropriate to the fulfillment of those objectives. If we say that two years of a general education program beyond the high school are desirable for all high school graduates, then it follows that society should find the means to make such educational opportunity available. On the other hand, let us assume that it is agreed that higher education should seek some less extensive goal. The choice then seems to be two-fold. One possible purpose may be to educate an intellectual elite in order that our society may have a cadre of persons who will preserve and advance knowledge for its own sake, as a personal adornment and as a cultural monument. Presumably, a society which desires to perpetuate such an intellectual elite will find the appropriate institutional mechanisms needed to accomplish this end. An alternative purpose may be to educate individuals to meet definite manpower requirements of our society for professional and para-professional personnel. This purpose must involve some planning which inter-relates educational programs and manpower developments.

If we accept something less than a general objective for higher education, we are then confronted with the problem of student selection. How do we propose to determine which high school graduates shall have access to higher education? Here the choices are to establish certain intellectual and economic standards of selection or to provide open access and to let actual competition at the higher education level determine who shall obtain graduation and placement in professional employment. There are questions of efficiency involved in this choice, but there are questions of human values involved as well. These are basic policy issues.

THE HISTORICAL BACKGROUND
OF HIGHER EDUCATION

Before I undertake to enumerate certain planning problems of higher education in the United States, let me digress somewhat in order to provide the proper social and institutional background for such a discussion. There are historians and other intellectuals today who proclaim that the United States of America constitutes a unique civilization and culture. Personally, I agree with this judgment. In religious terms, we of the United States have inherited a Judeo-Christian tradition. In intellectual terms, we have inherited a Graeco-Roman concept of knowledge and practice. In political terms, we have inherited an English common law and constitutional tradition, modified by the French Enlightment of the Eighteenth Century. Socially, we have accumulated widely diverse peoples of different ethnic, economic, social, and cultural patterns of behavior. In economic terms, we have built on our own resources and some foreign capital in response to the amazing abundance of the New World. The amalgam of all these influences, together with the ecology of America, has produced a unique civilization.

In this civilization, the institution of higher education has had a special place. When the first college was created in colonial America in 1636, it had a professional purpose: "to advance learning and perpetuate it to posterity; dreading to leave an illiterate ministry to the churches, when our present ministers shall lie in the dust." Most of the nine colonial colleges were intended to educate ministers or missionaries for the denominations of various religious groups. Soon, however, education for public service and law became equally important with education for the ministry. I once made a count of the professional occupation of the 1,000 graduates of Miami University in the years between 1826 and 1873. I found that one-third became ministers, one-third became lawyers, and the remaining one-third had engaged in a variety of professional endeavors from medicine and business management to journalism and military service. The point is that from the beginning of its history in America higher education has had a professional orientation.

Initially, the colonial college received a charter from the government of a royal or proprietary colony. Often the charter carried with it certain colonial patronage as well, since government and an established church were much inter-twined in colonial practice. Only with independence and the development of state governments did we begin in this country to make a differentiation between a private college and a public college. The distinction was clearly established by the famous Dartmouth College opinion of Chief Justice John Marshall of the United States Supreme Court in 1819. The public college created by state government differed little, however, from the privately sponsored college before 1860. It sometimes received a land-grant for its support, but seldom enjoyed continuing financial sustenance from the public purse. Both public and private colleges tended to be closely tied to various religious denominations. The way west was dotted with colleges as well as settlements.

In the years between the Civil War and World War I, two major trends appeared in the history of American higher education. One was the emergence of a new concept of higher education, labeled for convenience the emergence of the university. The second was a growing secularization of higher education, a decreasing preoccupation with religious purposes and practices. The American college was rigorously classical in its curriculum, providing a liberal education in the classical languages, rhetoric, natural philosophy, ethics, and history. This background of education was expected to be sufficient preparation for essentially on-the-job training in the ministry, law, medicine, and other professions. The American university after 1865 moved in two new directions. From Germany it imported the idea of graduate study and research, with its emphasis upon scholarship in depth and the exploration of new knowledge. In addition, the American university began its orientation professionally in terms of specific programs, such as colleges of engineering, of agriculture, of law, of teacher education, of medicine, of business, and of journalism. Moreover, with the federal government's passage of the Morrill Act in 1862 and with post-war expansion of state government expenditures, the public university became increasingly visible on the American higher education scene. At the same time, the private college and the private university began to loosen or cut their ties with religious bodies. None of these events occurred at any one time, nor were these developments fully accomplished by 1915. But these were the major thrusts of higher education in America between 1865 and our involvement in World War I.

The period from 1918 to 1939 was one of growth for American higher education, complicated by the agonizing experience of ten years of economic depression. The trends of the fifty years from 1865 to 1915 came to fruition in these years. The proportion of the college-age population enrolling in higher education increased from under nine percent to just over fifteen percent; the number of students expanded from 600,000 to 1.5 million. Under the impact of depression, the enrollment of public colleges and universities grew more rapidly than that of the private colleges and universities. The curriculum became ever more clearly related to the needs of preparation for professional practice. The advancing industrialization of the American economy began to change manpower requirements, and depression gave impetus to youth to seek education as an alternative to unemployment. The American university was seeking to advance knowledge but still found its intellectual stimulation in Western Europe.

In the last thirty years since 1940 American higher education has undergone profound change. Higher education has entered a period of maturity as an institution of our society. This development began when a beleaguered nation turned to American universities for assistance in meeting the challenge of war. American scholars, assisted by refugees from Europe, responded in notable fashion. Research became the principal university function of the war years, while colleges and universities turned their attention to the education of military officers and of scientists and engineers needed in the war effort. After the conclusion of World War II, research supported by the federal government remained as a major university endeavor. Economic growth and the attainment of maximum employment became national goals to which higher education became a principal contributing agent. The conflict of cold war and the evidence of scientific and technological advancement by the Communist nations made higher education vitally important as an instrument of national survival. The end of this current era is not in sight, although the fortunes of higher education have become enmeshed with the complexities of financing our national defense and of achieving varied social goals.

HIGHER EDUCATION

AS A SOCIAL INSTITUTION

In the process of undergoing this historical experience, American higher education has acquired certain definite characteristics as a social institution. First of all, higher education has become a vitally important institution. Until 1915 the United States was developed economically by individual effort based upon personal initiative, personal courage, and personal brawn. When the business coroporation became increasingly the instrument of personal endeavor, masses of unskilled labor, largely imported from Europe and to some extent from Asia, were added. Very little of this economic effort depended upon the accumulated knowledge or professional skills transmitted by the American college and university. Today, all this is changed. The business corporation no longer needs masses of unskilled workmen. Instead it needs the scientists, engineers, managers, specialists, and technicians provided by higher education. Government service, and especially our national defense, require more and more educated individuals. The American public expects more health care and more services of many kinds which can be provided only by an enlarged number of professional practitioners. And the educational establishment itself from pre-school to refresher institutes and workshops needs more persons to staff its own indispensable operation. Today, the welfare of America depends upon higher education, so much so that the President of the United States in a rare moment of non-harassment proposed that we call this the Age of Education.

Secondly, the American university is now the intellectual center of the Western world. No longer do we Americans look to Western Europe for our intellectual stimulation, guidance, and direction. The great advances in learning now take place in this country. We have inherited the mantle of Western learning, even as we have acquired the unenvied task of political leadership of the Western world. More than our own national survival is at stake in the performance of American higher education.

In the third place, American higher education is the instrumentality of social mobility in our society. For three hundred years the American ethic proclaimed that the individual could advance his own status in society by hard work, and a little bit of luck. It is not important to note the exceptions or qualifications to this belief. It is enough to observe that for substantial numbers of persons the American dream was realizable through individual endeavor. Now the American dream has a different prerequisite; it still depends upon individual endeavor, but it requires formal education as well. The principal avenue of social mobility has become education, and particularly higher education.

In the fourth place, American higher education as an institution continues to reflect the circumstances of a federal system of political government and of a pluralistic social structure. Federalism as a framework of government no longer means in our country a division of governmental functions between a central government and fifty constituent governments. Rather, federalism means a sharing of governmental endeavors, with the interest of one government preponderant in some fields such as foreign affairs and national security, and with the interest of the constituent governments supposedly predominant in matters of health, education, welfare, and public safety. Thus, public higher education in the United States means primarily colleges and universities created by state governments and directed by such arrangements as each separate state government may see fit to establish. Similarly, a pluralistic social structure permits a variety of enterprises within various broad types of social institutions. This pluralism is more than a matter of various churches, various colleges and universities, various labor unions, and various voluntary associations. It means, also, a very extensive, indeed predominant, private sector in the American economy.

Thus, American colleges and universities, over 2,200 in number, may be state or local government sponsored —only a few are sponsored by the federal government— or they may be sponsored by private groups. The colleges and universities under private sponsorship may be church-related or they may be non-sectarian in religious affiliation. Even the church-related college or university in this country today may be increasingly independent of church control or church direction. In addition, American colleges and universities may receive financial support from a variety of sources: students, government, individual benefactors, private business corporations, private foundations, and church bodies. The federal government, for example, in its support of higher education through research grants, facility grants and loans, student aid grants and loans, specialized instructional grants, equipment grants, developing institutional grants, and planning grants makes no distinction between the public and the private sponsorship of an individual college or university.

I dwell upon this history of higher education and upon these institutional characteristics of higher education because they so vitally affect the planning process in higher education. In a federal governmental structure and a pluralistic social structure, there is no single center of higher educational planning. Nor do we want any such center; at least I don't. Moreover, only as higher education has become more and more important in political and social terms, and more and more expensive in economic terms, has there been a growing demand that more attention be given to the planning process in higher education. Importance means that we in higher education must be more precise in the definition of our objectives and in the calculation of the appropriate means to ensure the realization of those objectives. The expense of our operation means that we must be more careful in the utilization of our resources than ever before. Such precision and such care can only be exercised through planning.

At the same time, it must be understood that this planning proceeds not alone within some 2,200 colleges and universities and through the voluntary associations of these colleges and universities. Higher education planning in America is also proceeding in many different administrative agencies of the federal government and in the administrative agencies of fifty different state governments.

THE PLANNING PECULIARITIES
OF HIGHER EDUCATION

Up to this point I have been outlining the general institutional context of higher educational planning in the United States. It is also useful, I believe, to say something about the peculiarities of the planning process within the individual college or university. There may have been a time within American colleges and universities when the planning activity could be identified primarily if not exclusively as the province of the administrative staff, if not of the president alone. It is fairly obvious that this is not the situation today. Faculties are demanding and asserting a major role in the determination of educational policies and plans. Presidents and their academic administrative associates including department heads may be leaders in the discussion and consideration of educational policies and plans, but faculties increasingly seem to expect that major issues will be decided by faculty vote. Even the delegation of authority to make decisions to faculty representatives in a faculty council is a suspect practice.

To this faculty role in academic planning must now be added a growing expectation on the part of students that they too will have an opportunity to participate in the preparation of plans. The academic community is a long ways from finding answers yet to the question of how effectively to structure student participation in academic planning, not to mention the question of how to define the proper scope of student concern with issues of academic objectives and procedures. None of us in the world of higher education doubts, however, that the phenomenon of student power is with us to stay, and that we must find ways and means of more effective involvement of students in the governance of our colleges and universities.

It is somewhat ironic that we should be experiencing enlarged faculty and student roles in academic planning at the same time when there is an enlarged planning operation affecting colleges and universities carried on by governments, voluntary associations, and others. Faculties and students alike have not yet caught up with the external facts of life which today influence the operation of individual colleges and universities.

There is another aspect of faculty and student participation in the planning of higher education which must receive greater attention than has yet been given to it. Planning is not concerned solely with goals and objectives. It is equally concerned with resources. No plan is an adequate guide to action unless it can be financed. There is little point other than the experience of the exercise itself in preparing plans which cannot be carried out within the limits of available financial resources. Most faculty members and students within a college or university favor independence of decision-making and enlarged expenditures. They almost never ask: where is the money to come from? or can we have both independence and affluence?

THE OBJECTIVES
OF HIGHER EDUCATION

The substantive issues of higher educational planning can be best discussed under four headings:

1. Objectives
2. Enrollment
3. Programs
4. Resources

It is customary to describe the purposes or goals of higher education as being three in number: instruction, research, and public service. This description is adequate but also misleading, since it confuses process and objective. Instruction is a process, the educated graduate is an objective. Research is a process; addition to knowledge is an objective. Public service is a process; services actually performed are the objective.

In planning its objectives, an individual college or university needs to do more than assert a commitment to instruction, research, and public service. Each of these categories of higher education activity raises various important issues for decision.

Public service is a not too well defined category of activity. I personally like to think of public service as involving primarily the work of continuing education. In addition, public service embraces consultation about the application of knowledge to specific public or private problems, technical assistance to government agencies, and the provision of clinical services in connection with a medical school or other instructional activity. In general, the prevailing practice of American higher education has been to render such public service as might be requested from an individual college or university, and as funds for such service might be provided.

The best known of all continuing education programs of American higher education has been the agricultural extension service operated in conjunction with our colleges of agriculture in Morrill Act land-grant state universities and encouraged by federal financial assistance since 1914. The success of this endeavor has produced many proposals for some kind of "urban" extension service and finally influenced the provisions of Title I of the Higher Education Act of 1965. Another aspect of continuing education has been the teacher in-service institutes in science and engineering stimulated by grants of the National Science Foundation and the similar teacher institutes authorized by Title V of the National Defense Education Act of 1958. The development of the concept of "public television" as advanced by the recent Carnegie Commission on Educational Television and embodied in the Public Broadcasting Act of 1967 represents still another approach.

Continuing education may be general in scope, intended to provide instruction in the cultural characteristics or in the public affairs of our own society or other societies. Or continuing education may be more specifically oriented to particular professional fields, endeavoring to provide an up-dating of knowledge and skill in engineering, business management, public administration, school teaching, medicine, law, and other fields. The means of instruction may be by television, radio, periodic conferences, seminars, workshops, and institutes.

Beyond the realm of continuing education as such, there are consulting services, foreign technical services, and clinical services which a college or university may be asked to perform or desire to perform. Personally, I have certain reservations about the provision of consulting services by a college or university directly, although it is quite common for universities to provide educational consulting service to local public schools through their colleges of education, to offer some testing service through an engineering station of a college of engineering, and business reporting service through a college of business. In general, I think it is more appropriate for a college or university to have a policy encouraging faculty members as individuals to engage in consulting services than for the college or university to operate consulting services as such. Foreign technical services have been undertaken by colleges and universities under contract with the Agency for International Development and its predecessors. Insofar as clinical services are concerned, important as these are in connection with medical education and other programs, we in college and university administration have learned that they are also expensive to operate.

There is no doubt that public service is an important and indeed expanding area of higher education activity. The needs are growing, and federal legislation, including the State Technical Services Act of 1965, indicates a rising expectation that colleges and universities should undertake more such effort. The Carnegie Foundation for the Advancement of Teaching has recently published a pamphlet reprinted from its 1966-67 annual report entitled: "The University at the Service of Society." This pamphlet should be required reading for all facutly and administrative committees or individuals who are engaged in planning the role of a particular college or university in this field of public service.

So much has been written about the research activities of higher education in recent years that it is almost impossible to think of anything new to say on the subject. As I have indicated in my historical sketch above, research became a major activity of American higher education only about thirty years ago, during World War II. We all hear frequently the charge that college and university faculties are more interested in research than in teaching and that research activity has corrupted the financial condition and the academic integrity of American higher education. While there may be some basis in fact for these accusations, I am inclined to believe that they are exaggerated and that they fail to recognize the importance of this research activity. Without question, the growth of university research activity has encouraged faculty members to give greater attention than before 1940 to graduate instruction and to organized research projects. The fact that federal funds on an increasingly generous basis up until a year ago were available for research helped to promote this situation. Moreover, faculty reputations *outside* the particular college or university where the faculty member serves tend to be based upon the evidences of productive scholarship. This fact has also helped to stimulate greater faculty interest in research endeavor.

I happen to be one of those individuals who believes that instruction and research are complementary rather than conflicting characteristics of scholarship. I recognize that research is more closely integrated with graduate study than undergraduate instruction, and I know from personal observation that some faculty members have greater gifts as instructors than as researchers, and vice versa. In many universities the neglect of undergraduate instruction, if it has indeed taken place, has resulted from more complicated circumstances simply than the growth of research activity. We have lacked the manpower resources to staff both the instruction and research activities of universities with senior or top-flight scholars, and we have lacked the financial resources to achieve a desirable balance. Beyond this, I think it may be accurate to assert that instructional procedures at the undergraduate level in our universities have not been given the careful and the innovative attention they deserve.

At more and more universities more careful planning is now being devoted to the whole subject of undergraduate instruction. In a recent report of a committee on undergraduate education published by one of our leading public universities, the chapter discussions, and the numerous recommendations of the committee, are presented under such headings as admission of the undergraduate student, the quality of teaching, the academic climate, liberal and general education, major fields of study, the honors college, student advising, and organization of undergraduate instruction. Here we are moving into details of program planning, but it is surely clear that such program planning can only be undertaken within the context of some definite instructional objectives of the university.

My plea is the standard one for careful and clear delineation of desired objectives in instruction, research, and public service. These objectives should be formulated in some detail, should be evaluated and reviewed periodically, and should be revised or reformulated from time to time. Such objectives insofar as instruction is concerned should establish the goals for the general and specialized programs of instruction and the framework of personal values to be achieved in the process of such instruction. The objectives of the student life activity of the college or university need to be integrated with these instructional objectives. Similarly, careful consideration needs also to be given to the research and public service objectives of the college or university. A college or university plan has not been developed until these objectives are specified with some degree of precision and clarity.

ENROLLMENT

The second major part of a college or university plan must deal with enrollment. Here the issues revolve around questions of quantity and quality. It is my general impression that today many public institutions are much preoccupied with the matter of how to restrict enrollment and that some private institutions are much concerned with the matter of how to increase enrollment.

In part, these concerns reflect factors of price and of available resources.

The whole question of quantity is more than a matter of economics, and deserves much more extensive consideration than it often receives. If the objectives of higher education instruction are primarily to meet the manpower requirements of our society, then our planning should proceed with some caution. Moreover, much of such planning will have to be done beyond the walls of a single college or university. We have been fortunate in the United States in that the demand for educated talent has generally outrun the supply. Shortly after the end of World War II, Seymour Harris, in his *The Market for College Graduates* predicted an excess supply of college graduates within the next ten years. If the composition and structure of the American labor market had remained static, this forecast might indeed have been accurate. As events would have it, this nation has experienced a continuing shortage rather than a surplus of educated talent in the past twenty years. The prospect is for a continuing shortage over the next twenty years as well.

In countries with a Spanish colonial tradition or background, I have been impressed by the large number of lawyers and accountants graduated by their universities. But once it is made clear that students are enrolled largely on a part-time basis and that government service tends to be the major occupation where these universities were located, the situation was understandable. The situation was also a warning that it is possible to provide more educated talent of certain kinds than a nation needs or can readily absorb. Indeed, it is not out of the realm of possibility that we have in the United States now all the law schools we need to produce the educated legal talent required in our society. On the other hand, we face sizable deficits in our supply of educated talent in the various health professions.

There are two complications in this concern for the manpower requirements in the American labor force. One is the higher education of women. The other is the concept of higher education for citizenship. It is difficult to discuss either of these subjects without saying the wrong thing, or without opening one's self to considerable misunderstanding. I see no reason why women should not have the same higher education opportunities available to men, but I also believe that it is contrary to experience to expect women to enter the professional labor market in the same numbers or with the same intentions as men. At the same time, I do not consider the time and funds devoted to women's education to be wasted. Many women will make good use of their education in family and community life. In addition, many women will be in and out of the professional labor market, depending upon family needs and circumstances. This situation should help our society to cope with the peaks and valleys of market demand for professional talent.

A major argument in favor of elementary and secondary education in this country since the days of Thomas Jefferson has been that the citizens of a republic and of a democracy must be literate. Today, it is often said that amid the complexities of contemporary society the citizen ought to have at least two years of education beyond the high school. Personally, I am not overly impressed by this citizenship argument. I am sure that literacy is a prerequisite for citizenship in a democracy, but I remain unconvinced that such minimum literacy as should be the common achievement of all youth in this country cannot be accomplished in twelve years of formal schooling. To add another two years to such inadequacies as may have been experienced in the preceding twelve years may be helpful in postponing entry into the labor market but scarcely constitutes education for citizenship.

Under the heading of programs, I wish to say something about the concept of general education as a part of higher education. It may well be asked whether all youth ought not to be exposed to the benefits of general education within the framework of higher education. I can only answer this question briefly, but emphatically, from my own definition of general education and from my own point of view. That answer is NO!

The question of quality in higher education enrollment is necessarily related to the matter of quantity. If we assume that higher education involves a certain competence in intellectual ability and a certain level of achievement in intellectual performance, then the question of quality is one of definition and of identification. I happen to believe that one of the great strengths of American higher education is the variety of definitions which our numerous colleges and universities have set for themselves, and the broad scope they have provided for identification of those who would evidence the required abilities and standards of performance. But within this variety I think there has always remained a certain floor of minimum expected compenence.

No matter how imprecise may be our definition of that level of ability and achievement required by higher education in our country, our procedures for identifying those persons who possess this competence are equally inexact. Standardized tests of ability and achievement have made an outstanding contribution in enabling a nation-wide comparison of young people who are the product of 25,000 different school districts. But test scores are not an infallible indication of competence, and tell us very little about individual motivation or mental balance. The comparison of individuals upon the basis of test scores and high school records has led some colleges and universities to believe that the more top-flight students they obtain, the higher will be the quality of instruction the faculty will offer. What is so often overlooked in this kind of planning is the high degree of competition and even of frustration which may develop amid a group of persons of high intellectual competence. A student body of highly selected composition may indeed be an artificial or uncommon body of individuals of homogeneous talent ill-prepared later to work effectively in other groups of more diversified abilities.

Today, many persons are asking two questions about

individual abilities. First, do we have reason to believe that intellectual ability in an individual is an inherent characteristic not subject to change or development? The prevailing answer to this question on a matter where our knowledge is still imperfect seems to be that intellectual ability can be developed. The second question is whether or not intellectual ability as it is frequently defined today is relevant to all the instructional objectives of higher education. My own strong belief is that higher education is by definition a purpose and process based upon a certain minimum requirement of intellectual ability and performance. We might well do more than we do today in our society to give the inherent intellectual capacity of every individual an opportunity to develop. We will not, I think, find the appropriate way to eliminate social, cultural, and economic inequalities affecting education by removing the intellectual standards of higher education.

PROGRAMS

The instructional objectives of higher education are divided into discrete parts. Research and public service activities are divided into projects. These constitute the programs of a college or university. These programs may be classified first of all by subject matter areas: general education, technical education, the disciplines (the humanities, the social sciences, the biological sciences, the physical sciences, and mathematics), and professional fields of study (teacher education, business administration, engineering, architecture, art, music, nursing, law, dentistry, medicine, theology, etc.). These programs may also be classified by level of study: lower division (or two-year programs), baccalaureate programs, master's degree programs, doctoral degree programs, and graduate-professional programs.

Each of these programs deserves extensive consideration both by subject matter areas and by levels. For example, ever since 1920 the desirable content of a general education program has been under active discussion in American higher education. Daniel Bell's volume, *The Reforming of General Education,* published in 1966, is a noteworthy successor to the justly famous Harvard report of 1946, *General Education in a Free Society,* but at the same time it is only one title in a great array of literature on this subject. Few "higher educators" have resisted the temptation to explicate their own ideas on the subject of general education; this fact is attested by my five-foot bookshelf on this subject, including one of my own. It is enough here to say simply that general education is a program which continues to defy the best efforts of college and university faculties to find a viable, effective endeavor. We continue to hold to the objective of a broadly educated individual, but we in American higher education cannot formulate a program to accomplish this goal which will receive general acceptance. I know of no other program area in American higher education where every faculty has a greater opportunity for individual planning and decision-making than here.

Technical education is one of the great wastelands of American higher education. The concept of two-year programs to produce para-professional individuals in engineering technologies, business technologies, and health technologies seems to have been explored primarily by community colleges, although some of our urban-located universities have moved in the same direction. Since community colleges were so often organized and developed by local school boards under laws supervised by state boards of education, technical education has been confused with vocational education, and in some instances has acquired the unfortunate connation of second-rate endeavor which has so hampered vocational education. When the federal government entered this field with Title VIII of the National Defense Education Act, amended and extended by the Vocational Education Act of 1963, this confusion was only compounded.

Technical education should be considered an integral part of higher education and the importance of this program should receive more recognition than has been given it by our colleges and universities. A technical education program need not and should not be a terminal program. A technical education program can meet many manpower requirements, however, which do not necessitate a full baccalaureate program.

There has been a steady trend in American higher education in recent years to expand at the graduate level. In the professional education of school teachers, there is a rising expectation that more and more persons will continue their formal education through the master's level. There are new proposals for the professional degree in engineering to be awarded at the master's level. A number of university schools of business are now graduate schools and at those universities where undergraduate education in business remains extensive a graduate program is being added. Law is now exclusively a graduate-professional field of study requiring the baccalaureate as a prerequisite. Theology has adopted a similar arrangement, and increasingly medicine and dentistry are doing the same. In most scientific fields, such as the professional practice of chemistry, the acquisition of at least a master's degree is usually expected as the basis for professional recognition. The consequence of these and similar developments is a steady pressure for colleges and universities to expand their graduate programs.

Instructional programs within higher education involve more than the determination of certain broad instructional objectives and of more specific program content. The planning of any instructional program must also include a strategy of learning and a technology or process of performance. It is in these two areas of planning, I believe, where American higher education tends to be most deficient. Every field of study, whether that of a discipline or of professional practice, involves a theory of knowledge and a skill of communication or practice. The difficulty is that this theory of knowledge is more often implicit rather than explicit and must be discovered as a kind of by-product of the instructional process. A theory of knowledge ought to be clear-cut and ought to serve as a continuing guideline if program purposes are to be fully realized. Moreover, knowledge is a kind of inert property until it is communicated, discussed, analyzed, criticized, and otherwise carefully examined. In a professional field, practice is even more important than knowledge, and skill in the application of knowledge and experience is essential.

In addition, the technology of learning is an art which in most of our colleges and universities is still in a very primitive state. In the instructional process, we assume the presence of four major components: a scholar, a learner, a subject, and a skill of application. In some fashion these four ingredients must be integrated into a process of technology which produces at the conclusion of the production period a learner who has mastered the subject matter content and the skill of utilization desired by the scholar. The prevailing technology of this production process seems to be a scholar who lectures; a student who listens, reads, writes, experiments in a laboratory, and occasionally discusses; and a body of knowledge and skill usually embodied in books and the scholar's mind. For reasons of economy of effort, the scholar usually performs his part of this learning process with a group of students which we label a class. For reasons of tradition and convenience, we divide the production process into time periods, credit hours, and proficiency grades.

Today, there seems to be a growing interest in the

possibility that somehow we might improve this production process. There are many who think the prevailing production process is very much in the handicraft stage and that it could be updated and made vastly more efficient and economical. Unfortunately, we devote few of the resources of higher education to research and development designed to improve this production process. Faculty members frequently resist any proposals for change. And some proposals, initially at least, would involve sizable commitments of funds to new capital equipment such as teaching machines, computers, audiovisual materials, and learning packages which our financially hard-pressed colleges and universities cannot provide.

There have also been proposals which would provide more individualized instruction. Unfortunately, most of us are familiar with only a limited number of learning situations: the classroom, the seminar, the laboratory, and the tutorial. If one of the colleges or universities were to seek to substitute more tutorial instruction for classroom instruction, again cost factors would become almost prohibitive. A different kind of proposal looks to more individual initiative or participation by the learner in this productive process. Almost all such proposals are related to new uses of machines or equipment, and, as I have just noted, these may be quite expensive. Still other proposals look to the organization of new teaching procedures involving an instructional technician, an academic assistant, a staff instructor, and a senior scholar.

To some extent, in our universities with our use of teaching assistants we are attempting a differentiation of skills in the instructional process. One difficulty is that most senior scholars are defined and identified in terms of research productivity and not in terms of instructional productivity.

There is an urgent need for more research and development of the production process utilized in our instructional programs, and for more innovation and planning to improve this process. The time for improvements is long overdue.

RESOURCES

While it is convenient for the purpose of analysis to divide the concerns of the planning process in higher education into various parts, I would emphasize the inter-relationship which exists between the planning of objectives, enrollment, programs, and resources. No part of this inter-relationship is more critical than the matter of resources. It is characteristic of American higher education always to operate in an institutional environment in which aspirations and ambitions outrun available resources. I myself do not expect ever to experience any other circumstance.

As this was written the president of one of our outstanding universities told me that in his university it had been necessary to fix enrollment quotas at the master's degree level, at the doctoral degree level, and at the graduate-professional level for every discipline and every professional field of study. Moreover, once established, these enrollment quotas could be exceeded only upon his personal approval. This administrative practice simply represents good management. It represents careful planning which inter-relates the objectives, enrollment, programs, and *resources* of that particular university.

We may collect a whole library on higher education as an institution and for individual colleges and universities, yet I am continually amazed to find how often various persons in the federal government and in colleges and universities ignore one of the fundamental financial facts of life. This fact is the distinction to be observed between the current operating resources and the capital resources of higher education. Income is not just indiscriminate; it is either operating income or capital income; it is either income with which to finance the operations during a fiscal period or income for investment in plant, equipment, endowment, or loan funds. Our planning and our financial management in higher education is deficient unless we distinguish clearly between our operating accounts and our capital accounts.

Next is the importance of integrating the income and expenditure categories of current operations. The so-called "bible" which sets up the standards for financial reporting of higher education in this country prescribes a three-fold grouping of current expenditures. I believe that a five-fold grouping would be more realistic and meaningful: instruction and general, research, public service, auxiliary services, and student aid. It is improper as well as undesirable not to indicate clearly the separate sources of income made available for each of these five major activities of colleges and universities.

For example, federal government grants are made for research, public service, and student aid. These grants cannot legally be used for other activities, and this fact should be indicated clearly in the current operating statements and in the financial planning of each college or university. Almost no grants are made by the federal government to assist the instructional activity as such, and this is another fact which should be made absolutely evident.

It is only when we recognize that much of the income of a college or university is earmarked or dedicated income and that such income is available only for specified activities that we shall be able to obtain a full understanding of the realities of resource management in a college or university. There is something improper in charging all students an instructional fee and utilizing part of this income for financial assistance to a few. I know all of the rationalizations for this practice, and I consider them inadequate. It would be far more proper, I think, to charge a differential instructional fee to students based upon size of family income. But whatever the decision on this matter, we need to handle income receipts more carefully than we sometimes do, and we need to understand as well as plan the different uses which must be made of available income.

Still a third observation has to do with the introduction of a planning-programming-budget system in higher education. There has been a good deal of talk about PPBS in government and in business in recent years, but very little discussion of the application of such a system to higher education. We cannot long delay the adoption of this new tool of fiscal planning and management.

Budgeting practice in most colleges and universities is decidedly outmoded. Very few colleges and universities have a program budget. Colleges and universities budget expense and income by organizational units—primarily the instructional departments and colleges—and by objects of expenditure such as personal services, supplies and equipment, fringe benefits, travel, utility services, and contractual services. A program budget does not discard this concern with organizational units or objects of expenditure, but it subordinates these phases of budgeting to the program units of the college or university. Moreover, program budgeting indicates the outputs of expenditure.

I have already indicated the major program components of the instructional activity of a college or university: general education, technical education, various specialized disciplines and undergraduate professional fields of study, the master's program, the doctoral program, and graduate-professional programs. I know that a single instructional department in a university may undertake parts of many different programs. A department of physics, for example, may be involved in general education, a baccalaureate physics program, a master's physics program, a doctoral physics program, one or more research projects, and one or more public service projects. This is not an unusual situation. But the planning and the management within the physics department of a university needs to know its work load and output in each of these programs, its personnel and other input requirements in order to meet these program objectives, and the financial resources available to its for conducting these programs.

Furthermore, programs cannot be defined just in terms of departments. Programs extend across department lines and must be directed and coordinated as such. Thus, the general education program of a college or university is not the exclusive endeavor of a department of physics. The department may contribute personnel and other inputs to this program, but it does so in concert with other departments. Programs extend beyond departmental boundary lines, and important as departments are organizationally they cannot be planned or managed as program units but only as constituent parts of programs.

One last general comment about resources planning is that most professional practitioners, business leaders, and political leaders believe the management of colleges and universities to be quite inefficient. I have tried frequently to point out that colleges and universities are not structured like a business corporation or even a government department. I have tried to point out that within the academic community power is shared by faculties, students, and administration. I have tried to point out that colleges and universities are subject to varied expectations from alumni, parents, social groups, government, and others. No matter how one tries to explain the differences, I find that no explanation ever overcomes the initial belief in inefficiency.

We in higher education—administrators, faculty, and students—are going to have to give a great deal more attention to our management of resources as a means of demonstrating our effectiveness in performing the operations we undertake and in realizing the objectives and program goals we set for ourselves. Most people contend that colleges and universities are always claiming to be broke, are always begging for more money, and are always claiming how much more they could accomplish if only they had more gifts or more tax funds. We are constantly told that there must be something wrong in this kind of situation. I agree that there is something wrong, but I fail to see any ready means of escape. One approach is to be more efficient in the planning and management of our resources.

CONCLUSION

Higher education planning has a vast frame of reference. It is no field of effort for the faint-hearted, the traditionalist, the opportunist. Higher education planning calls for dedicated effort, an innovative spirit, and optimism. Higher education planning is central to the further advancement of higher education activity.

Planning, as I noted at the outset, gives promise of no miracles. Planning as a process is no guarantee of effective plans, plans whose objectives are desirable, whose programs are sound, whose resources are adequate. But planning is a procedure for bringing organized intelligence to bear upon problems. Since we don't lack for problems in higher education, we have ample scope for planning.

When I was an Army officer in the Pentagon in World War II, my commanding general had a slogan with which he was very much taken. This slogan went something like this: "Any intelligent action taken today is preferable to delay in search of a perfect solution tomorrow." In a sense, this slogan is an appropriate one for a planner.

There is seldom a perfect solution to any problem. There are only preferable or reasonable or intelligent lines of action taken by men who realize that time is short, the burdens are many, the challenges never-ending, the expectations great, the opportunities demanding, the prospects hopeful. Planning is an indispensable part of decision-making. Planning without action is fruitless. Action without planning is dangerous. These lessons managers in many different kinds of enterprise have learned from experience. We in higher education must continually demonstrate that we have learned the lesson, too.

A Systems Analysis
of the University

During the past twenty-five years a good deal of attention has been given to the study of particular enterprises or organized entities as systems. A systems analysis has many advantages over more traditional studies of organizational structure or of the objects of budget expenditure.

A systems analysis focuses attention upon the objectives of an enterprise, and then concentrates concern upon the input factors and the dynamic process involved in the realization of these objectives. When systems analysis is combined with cost effectiveness determinations and with a planning-programming-budget sequence, decision-makers in an enterprise have a more thorough grasp of their whole endeavor than is otherwise available to them. A good part of our progress in recent years in building an "administrative science" has depended upon more effective methods of achieving an understanding of the administrative process. A systems analysis has provided us with a more realistic conception of how an enter-

71

prise operates and of what an enterprise accomplishes with its available resources and technology.

As already suggested, a systems analysis of an enterprise is concerned with three major parts: the input elements, a process of operation, and the desired outputs. A system in an enterprise is thus structured in much the same way as a system for computer analysis, which likewise consists of inputs, process, and outputs. In this approach the major concern is always with the desired outputs. The inputs and the process are simply methods or activities for achieving a given set of objectives.

Those who have studied any enterprise or organization of some historical duration are well aware that many an enterprise has begun with only an indefinite or vague formulation of desired outputs. Frequently, an enterprise develops, modifies, and even radically changes its objectives in the course of time, circumstances, experience, and varied leadership. Regardless of this historical perspective, systems analysis endeavors to find out what the objectives are as currently perceived and seeks to relate these desired outputs to a present set of inputs and a present process. Systems analysis may contribute to efficiencies in the accomplishment of objectives or to reformulation of objectives in terms of available inputs (or resources) or of available process (or technology). Systems analysis does not pretend to tell decision-makers what an enterprise ought to accomplish. It can only seek to assist the decision-makers in relating means to ends.

A systems analysis gains in reality to the extent that

inputs, process, and outputs can be expressed in quantitative terms. Some persons have gone so far as to assume that a systems analysis is of little utility unless all three basic parts of the system can be enumerated in some way. Undoubtedly, there are advantages in constructing a systems analysis in quantitative terms, but there may be difficulties in arriving at a satisfactory quantification of some phases of an enterprise. Sometimes the quantities may be quite different in characteristic—the apples, oranges, and bananas complication—and sometimes important parts of a system cannot very well be expressed in quantitative terms.

Systems analysis does serve a useful purpose whether or not the system can be expressed in satisfactory numerical language. It may be useful for persons within an enterprise or outside it to see the endeavor in terms of its systems components. And with some ingenuity over a period of time a surprisingly large part of the whole system may be describable in quantitative units.

A SYSTEMS ANALYSIS OF
A UNIVERSITY

If we accept the proposition that there are enterprises in our economy, in our government, and in our military establishment which have benefited from systems analysis, then we may well inquire whether or not there might be some advantage to a systems analysis of a university. The question obviously cannot be answered until we experiment with the approach.

To be sure, to those who think of higher education as a mystique beyond rational inquiry and understanding, then any systems analysis of a university as an enterprise is worthless, or even dangerous. Indeed, systems analysis may be regarded as just another bureaucratic procedure bent upon dehumanizing society and one of its great humanistic institutions, higher education. Increasingly today there are voices raised insisting that a university must not be thought of in "scientific" terms but rather in artistic and moral terms.

I am not suggesting at all that a systems analysis is necessarily the final word in seeking to understand the university. I propose only that a systems analysis may be worthy of experimentation in order to see if it does provide us with some new knowledge or some new wisdom about a very important enterprise in our society.

PROPOSED ANALYSIS

The first problem in undertaking a systems analysis of a university is to identify and classify the major factors or elements to be included in the basic threefold components of a system: the inputs, the process, and the outputs.[1] The chart which accompanies this discussion graphically presents the attempt to show a university as

1. I wish to acknowledge the stimulation to my own thinking on this subject resulting from a conference held in Princeton in 1963 under the leadership of John J. Corson, consultant to Carnegie Corporation of New York, and especially to the presentation of a project of study along these lines then being conducted at the

a system. The boxes on the left hand side of the chart identify the major inputs, the boxes in the center represent the major parts of the university process, and the boxes on the right hand side of the chart represent the major outputs. This proposed representation of the university as a system needs some explanation.

There are two general problems, however, which should be given some attention at the outset. One is the problem of quantitative enumeration. The other is the problem of financing. Should a systems analysis only include items which can sooner or later be quantified? Any such limitation for a university would be quite restrictive and has been rejected here. In addition, it has seemed essential in the systems analysis of a university to give some emphasis to the overriding importance of financial considerations. Ordinarily, it is customary to express the inputs of a system in terms of physical quantities, such as people or man hours, equipment, and plant. But in higher education the limiting factor always is the budget for current operating purposes. And while the physical plant available for current operations is another limitation, the financial resources for capital improvements determine the ability to expand this capacity. It has seemed imperative to find some way to include financial considerations as a major factor in attempting to chart a university system.

University of Pennsylvania. At the same time, it should be understood that I alone am responsible for the particular suggestions and views expressed herein.

THE UNIVERSITY
A SYSTEMS ANALYSIS

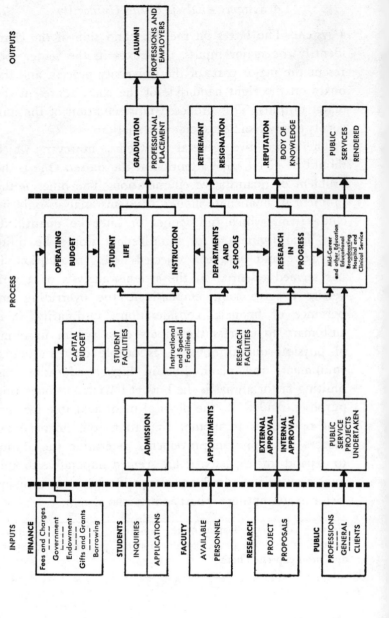

The major inputs of a university have been listed herein as finances, students, faculty, research ideas, and certain members of the general public who may seek university services. Within the box labeled "Finance," the various principal sources of funds for current operations and for capital improvements have been listed. The potential student body of a university is represented by the inquiries concerning possible admission and the actual number of applications for admission which a university may receive. The faculty input refers to the available supply of persons who might be appointed in a university, depending upon the established qualifications of education and experience, salary levels, and staffing standards. A fourth major input identified in the chart is possible or proposed research projects. These presumably will be developed by faculty members but may be initiated from sources external to the university itself. The fifth input is the general public from whom may be drawn clients of a university for mid-career education, for utilization of broadcasting services, and for consulting or clinical services.

In this listing of inputs I gave a good deal of thought to the question of including management or entrepreneurial talent as an important item. In economic analysis it has long been recognized that entrepreneurial talent is a vital input. Should this talent be considered less important in university analysis? Moreover, if finance is to be given a major emphasis in the systems analysis of a university, does not management deserve the same attention? After lengthy argument with myself, I eliminated management or entrepreneurial talent as a separate input for two reasons (other than some concern with simplicity of presentation). Management is, I believe, implied in any organized process of operation. For the purposes of systems analysis, I think we may take it as a given, along with the state of the technology. In addition, since management in a university must necessarily be preoccupied with matters of finance, I decided that I had in effect included the input of management when I listed finance as an input.

The construction of a chart representing the university as a process poses a number of complications. It seemed appropriate to emphasize four primary processes as essential parts of the university: student life, instruction, the conduct of research, and public service. But there were also four preliminary and important phases of the university process: the admission and enrollment of students, the selection and appointment of faculty, the approval (and financing) of particular research projects, and the determination of the public services to be offered. These processes necessarily precede student life, instruction, the prosecution of research, and the performance of public services. These processes in themselves seem sufficiently important to receive separate acknowledgment, even in a highly generalized representation of the university process.

In seeking to identify the most important parts of the university as a process, it seemed desirable to recognize academic departments and schools as a separate item. Faculty members, organized usually into working units of departments or schools, perform the work involved in the process of instruction, research, and public service. They may also be involved in matters of student life. The maintenance of this faculty resource in a state of productivity is a major element of the university process and should not be assumed simply as part of other processes. In addition, this faculty process has an identity of activity which deserves a good deal of emphasis. Hence, both appointment of faculty members and the operation of departments have been identified as essential elements of the university process.

When we turn to the problem of identifying the outputs of a university we encounter special difficulties. The obvious output, of course, is made up of graduates, or degrees conferred. To be sure, this is not an adequate indication of work accomplishment, since a better statement of work load would be credit hours of instruction provided. Yet, degrees awarded appear to be the principal objective of the instructional process, and for this reason it seemed necessary to recognize these as a primary output. With graduation, we have coupled professional placement as an output. Since higher education in our country is oriented to the preparation of graduates for professional employment, I think this output deserves much more attention than it often receives. Moreover, graduates become alumni and thus enter, it is hoped, into a continuing relationship with the university from which they have received their degree. But employers also have a continuing relationship with a university, since they are the "consumers" of the output of graduates.

Should a systems analysis include a faculty output as such, or do student graduates, research results, and public services rendered represent the only outputs we need to acknowledge from the faculty input? It seemed desirable to give some mention in the systems chart to the "use-up" of faculty resources in the forms of retirement and resignation. Turnover rates for faculty members tell us something about the university process, and retirement represents a separation from service with a continuing obligation presumably funded during the university process itself. Accordingly, the two items noted on the chart were included as an output traceable to the faculty input.

It is not easy to determine how to designate the research output. The two listed here clearly defy any precise quantification: (1) reputation of the institution, and (2) contributions to the current body of knowledge in a discipline or professional field. There is little doubt but that research accomplishments do contribute to the general reputation of a university, as periodic rating efforts clearly reveal. Contributions to knowledge, of course, constitute the accepted and expected result of research within a university.

Finally, the public service operation of a university is expected to result in various services rendered, such as professional practitioners who have been brought "up to date" in their practice, members of the public who have been assisted in continuing their general education through broadcasting, and clients who have received consulting service, medical service, or other service rendered by the university as a part of its endeavor. These public services appear to be more and more important under present conditions.

This summary of the chart presented herewith can only be suggestive. The chart endeavors to set forth certain inputs, certain processes, and certain outputs of a university. Other individuals might well organize and classify the major components of a university system in other ways and present such components in a somewhat different charting. This particular representation of a systems analysis of a university is not necessarily complete or beyond improvement.

THE UTILITY
OF SYSTEMS ANALYSIS

A systems analysis of a university may serve several useful purposes. First, the very analysis effort itself should help develop a clearer understanding of university operations than might otherwise be achieved. To some extent, the chart presented herein might assist this understanding for many persons: trustees, faculty, students, staff, alumni, and others. A systems analysis then becomes another kind of representation of the reality of a university. Secondly, a systems analysis of this kind, in part at least, does lend itself to quantification. Such enumeration, together with the use of appropriate statistical techniques of analysis, may provide useful information about university activities and procedures. In addition, systems analysis may help to provide certain insights into both university organization and university financing.

There is little need here to dwell upon the importance of achieving an understanding of the nature of the university enterprise. It is surprising that there should continue to be so much misinformation and misconception about an institution of such ancient and honorable lineage as higher education. Without reviewing the various failures in understanding, we may suggest that any approach which helps to dispel confusion about a university is worth the effort and that many different approaches including systems analysis seem desirable in order to promote better comprehension of the enterprise.

There are several parts of this systems analysis which do lend themselves to quantification. Universities generally maintain careful records about students, and these data can be translated readily into quantitative terms. The number of inquiries received about admission policies and standards, the number of actual applications received, the number of admissions issued, and the number of admissions actually enrolled—all of these data are usually available without difficulty. Enrollment in terms of full- and part-time students, in terms of credit hours, in terms of student status in progress toward a degree, and in terms of point averages or qualitative performance—these data are also usually available. Generally, there is little data about student life apart from some record about the residence of a student (living at home, living in a university residence hall, or living adjacent to the university). Moreover, exit or dropout records are usually non-existent, except for an enumeration of students dropped for reason of failure to maintain the required academic standard of performance. Universities maintain careful records of degrees awarded, and some maintain fairly good records of immediate placement. Alumni records are also kept, although inevitably some alumni are "lost" each year.

The implications of these student and instructional data are obvious to anyone familiar with the operations of a university and tell faculty, administrators, and others a great deal about the quality and the problems of a particular university.

Insofar as the faculty is concerned, the quantitative data are only partially available as a rule. The supply and the labor market characteristics of available faculty members are not too well known. There are occasional studies on this whole matter but little concrete information will exist at any one university. If a university has staffing standards and a carefully formulated staff budget, then the number of vacancies to be filled will be known. Some quantitative data may then be available about efforts at recruitment, the number of referrals considered, and the number of actual appointments.

Faculty positions by departments and other instructional units are almost always known, as well as the number of retirements and resignations by time periods. There is often a good deal less precise information available about the division of faculty resources between instruction, research, public service, and general university work. Also, it is not often known exactly what outside professional and other practice a faculty member may be engaged in.

The most important aspects of a faculty, however, are the qualitative judgments made about their achievements as teachers and as researchers. There seems to be very little which systems analysis techniques as we now know them can contribute to this phase of university operations. It is often said that research accomplishments are more readily determinable than teaching accomplishments. One may count the number of research grants received, research projects prosecuted, articles and books published, awards or other evidence of recognition received. There are qualitative implications to each such enumeration, but there is not necessarily a definite correlation between indications of activity and even of popularity in a profession and assurance of major contributions to knowledge.

The evaluation of instructional performance by faculty members has commanded a great deal of discussion but has produced little in the way of systematic, continuing procedure. As a consequence, there is almost nothing on this subject which can be incorporated into systems analysis. The most that may be achieved from systems analysis is to obtain quantitative data upon the utilization of faculty resources in relation to supply, in relation to various parts of the university process, and in relation to turnover. Such data would be worthwhile to have available in any university.

SYSTEMS ANALYSIS
AND ORGANIZATION STRUCTURE

One possible utility in systems analysis of a university is the contribution it may make to decisions about organization structure. The basic issues today about university organization are probably beyond the capacity of systems analysis to illuminate: the respective roles of authority to be exercised by boards of trustees and administrative officers, students, and faculty members. Indeed, it is likely that to some students and faculty members systems analysis will appear to be simply another device for belittling their status. Systems analysis has little to offer in resolving the issue of the distribution of power within the university, or in ensuring organizational capacity to make timely and effective decisions in the light of changing circumstances.

At the same time, systems analysis can be used to help promote the cause of rationality as against irrationality in discussions about organization structure. Organizational structure is a means to an end, and the organization of a university should facilitate the university process and should ensure realization of the intended outputs. It should be useful in clarifying ideas and suggestions about university structure if the participants in this discussion—faculty members, students, and administrators—would always keep the university system clearly in mind. It may well be that much of the argument about organization is in reality an argument about goals and about process.

When we move away from questions involving the location of power among contending groups within a university and questions involving the capacity of a university to be decisive, the most important issues of organization have to do with structural arrangements for performing the instructional, research, and public service activities of the university. One structural difficulty arises from the peculiar nature of instruction which involves different levels of study and different fields of study. Another difficulty arises from the close relationship which usually exists between instruction and research. Still a third difficulty arises from the dual impact of instruction and research upon the public service commitments of a university.

It is the faculty of a university which constitutes the personnel resource or input of the university and which enables the university to carry on the various processes of instruction, research, and public service. Furthermore, it is the faculty of a university which must necessarily make or largely influence many vital decisions about how these processes shall be organized and carried out. Yet the most important ingredient of these processes—the budgeting of capital and current operating resources—involves determinations of available income which are likely to be beyond the faculty power to decide. In a very real sense, faculty members of a university operate under an injunction to handle a given quantity of plant and equipment resources, supply and equipment funds, and salary funds in the best possible combination to produce the best attainable results from their instruction, research, and public service efforts.

A faculty must accordingly be organized into working units of the university enterprise in order to produce certain desired outputs of instruction, research, and public service. The structural questions are how to identify these working units and then how to achieve the desired coordination of these working units through some mechanism of supervision. It is not easy to find a satisfactory answer within a university to these two questions. A great deal of experimentation and a continuing shuffling of work units and of supervisory structure within various universities attests to the difficulties of finding satisfactory solutions.

Organizationally, there appear to be two possible approaches to structuring the university process. One is to establish working units of a university to perform all three processes of instruction, research, and public service. The other choice appears to be to establish working units of a university which will perform these processes of instruction, research, and public service more or less separate and distinct one from another.

It is not our intention here to consider in detail these alternative organizational arrangements or to review the experience of different institutions in devising an organizational structure for their activities. Our immediate interest is whether or not systems analysis can help to answer this issue of choice in constructing organizational work units. I believe systems analysis can help in one important way. A careful study of the university process will reveal that the choice is essentially that of having three faculties to perform three activities, each on a highly specialized and separate basis, or one faculty dividing its efforts in various proportions of time to perform three different processes. Obviously, the rational basis of choice is to select the arrangement which is most efficient in producing the desired outputs.

Efficiency can only be determined with precision when inputs and process can be stated in quantitative terms and can then be related to outputs. The process which produces the most outputs for a given quantity of input is the most efficient. This kind of quantitative comparison is difficult to determine in a university. But perhaps some combination of objective and subjective judgment can assist in this sort of organizational decision.

Personally, my own subjective judgment based upon experience and observation is that instruction, research, and public service in a university are closely intertwined. At most times the academic scholar is likely to be engaged in all three activities; only the proportion of effort tends to vary at different times. The academic scholar engages usually in some research or study in order to advance his effectiveness in instruction. When the academic scholar seeks to communicate his knowledge to others outside the university or engages in consultation about problems to which he can contribute some expertise, then he is performing public service. At the same time, by his contact with the "hard facts" of experience outside the university, the scholar advances his own capacity to instruct effectively and to make instruction relevant to experience outside a university. The scholar who only teaches and does no research or public service cannot long, I think, remain a scholar. If working units for instruction, research, and public service are constructed separate one from the other, I believe evidence will soon accumulate to indicate that this is an inefficient organizational arrangement and an ineffective process of operation insofar as quality of output is concerned.

If the organizational judgment of university decision-makers favors working units of departments and schools to perform all three activities of instruction, research, and public service, then it seems evident that the structure of supervision in a university must provide the necessary coordination of effort as needed to ensure that university-wide objectives in instruction, research, and public service are realized. This coordination can usually be achieved through colleges and through a vice-president for academic affairs with an appropriate central staff.

The complications of the instructional process resulting from the various levels of instruction will be considered further in connection with the discussion below of the budget problems of a university. We may note here that at the undergraduate level there are actually two different kinds of instruction. On the one hand, the introductory and core courses a department offers are often intended for the non-specialist, although these courses may also serve the beginning specialist. On the other hand, there are the specialized courses to be provided at the undergraduate level which afford the professional educational achievement expected for a baccalaureate. Both kinds of instruction, the general and the specialized, are important at the undergraduate level. Sometimes the educational importance of this general instruction is emphasized organizationally by the establishment of a general college as a coordinating structure. Separate colleges of the disciplines and colleges of professional study may then complete the structural arrangement. In other circumstances colleges may be set up with internal coordinating arrangements for general and specialized education at the undergraduate level.

Beyond the baccalaureate, there are graduate-professional and graduate programs of instruction to be provided by a university. These again require some organizational identification as well as coordination of related efforts. Such identification and coordination can be achieved by a separate graduate-professional college, as is customary in medicine, law, dentistry, theology, and other fields. Sometimes, as for departments which must provide both undergraduate and graduate instruction, a graduate school provides special identification for the graduate instruction and a graduate dean serves to coordinate common problems of admission standards, degree requirements, course offerings, student assistance and relations, and similar academic concerns.

Organizational structure within a university must somehow accommodate different levels of instruction by faculty members as well as different kinds of activity by faculty members such as instruction, research, and public service. A systems analysis should contribute at a minimum to a clearer understanding of both process and desired outputs of a university, and thereby help to resolve issues of organization structure in terms of efficient and effective utilization of inputs in the carrying out of the process needed to obtain desired outputs.

In a very real sense, the faculty of a university performs a dual role. However organized into working units (departments) and coordinating units (colleges), faculty members serve as managers of the vital personnel resource of the university which faculty members constitute, and faculty members perform the processes which achieve the desired outputs of a university. Faculty members, in other words, do the work of a university, and, at the same time, have a major part in recruiting, developing, and retaining their own selves as needed to do the work of a university.

Organizationally, this peculiar dual role of faculty members raises another issue. The utilization of faculty resources requires one kind of organizational structure to coordinate the instructional activities, research activities, and public service activities. Will this same organizational structure be adequate to coordinate activities of faculty personnel management, of providing, developing, and conserving the faculty resource as a vital input? This is a question which must be answered by specific arrangements in specific circumstances. But a systems analysis of a university as here outlined does at least underline this vital dual faculty role, as performers of the university process and as managers of the vital personnel resource of the university.

STUDENT LIFE

This is not the place to undertake an extensive discussion of the problems of student life within a university. Anyone who is informed about current thinking among student leadership groups on a university campus is well aware of the complaints about supervision of student life and of the arguments for student control of student life. It is impossible here to review these complaints and arguments.

There may be some utility, however, in reexamining student life in the context of the university as a system. Such a reexamination might very well address itself to a fundamental question: what phases or what aspects of student life are essential to the functioning of the university as a system? If we recognize that students are a major input resource of the university and if we recognize that student life has some identity of its own apart from the instructional process as such, then we must decide what constitutes the student life essential to the university process.

In responding to this query, we can recognize two extreme positions. One position would assert that the total life of a student—his housing, his health, his social activity, his recreation, his economic welfare—is an integral part of the university instructional process and cannot be separated from that process. The opposite position would assert that the university has no interest in student life except as it is intimately and necessarily related to the direct instructional process. This second position would conceive of the student's personal life as irrelevant to the university and would accept an interest in and concern with only the student's academic performance.

When one states these positions in this way, it becomes fairly evident to most persons concerned about the university as an enterprise of learning that neither extreme is realistic. It is impossible to believe that academic performance can be separated from the physical and mental health of a student. It is impossible to believe that academic performance can be separated from the economic welfare of a student, that is, his ability to cope with the personal expense of university study. It is impossible to believe that academic performance can be separated from the social environment or circumstances within which the student lives. Student power groups would have parents, university administrators, and university faculties accept the proposition that student life can somehow be kept distinct from student academic performance, or that students as a social group have the capacity based upon past learning and experience to direct their own student life in a way which will satisfactorily integrate with the required standards of academic performance.

The only realistic way of looking at student life would seem to be in relative terms, in terms of the degree of integration of student life with standards of academic performance which may be essential to both the university process and the desired university output. It may well be, moreover, that these relative terms or degrees of integration may vary at different stages in the academic life of the student, such as freshman-sophomore, junior-senior, and graduate. If such differentiation seems desirable and feasible, then presumably there will be some progression of individual responsibility for student life even as there is some progression of individual responsibility for academic performance as a student advances to higher levels of learning.

It would seem useful if the present dialogue with students could be shifted from a debate about power to a debate about the learning process within the university as a system. If some or a good proportion of students want to separate student life from the university process, we need to develop some understanding of what this will mean insofar as the instructional process and the learned output are concerned. To what extent is it realistic in terms of the process and objectives of the university to separate student life from a university context? In what ways and to what degree is it possible to develop a separation of student life from the university process and still maintain the integrity of the university process and output? These are vital questions and these deserve careful, considered responses. A systems analysis might well contribute substantially to such careful consideration.

Universities are today confronted with the urgent necessity of developing a planning-programming-budget system. On all sides we hear complaints that universities face a major financial crisis, that expenditure requirements are outstripping income resources, and that universities will shortly be unable to continue their essential activities for society. The difficulty with these cries of distress is that they are almost all general in nature. University spokesmen have not presented carefully developed facts about activities and programs in order to make clear the specific nature of the financial difficulties confronting various universities. Only a well formulated planning-programming-budget system within a university can provide the adequate factual base upon which to evaluate the exact nature of the present financial crisis and upon which to formulate possible alternatives of action.

Generally, we are given three or four explanations for the higher levels of expenditure experienced by all universities. First, there is the obvious fact of enrollment increases, of more students enrolled in many universities. Secondly, we are reminded of the continued pressures for larger faculty salaries, pressures generated by demands from business and industry and from government and competing universities for the scarce resource of faculty talent. In the third place, we are reminded that universities require much more expensive equipment of all kinds from atomic reactors and computers to electron microscopes and television in order to perform their instructional and research efforts. In the fourth place, there are rising costs of plant operation occasioned in part by inflation, in part by unionization of maintenance employees and the need to pay more adequate wages than in the past, and in part by increased consumption of electric power and other utilities. One university president reported recently that without any increase in the number of students enrolled at his particular university the operating budget in 1967 was three times larger than it was in 1950 and six times larger than it was in 1935.

The difficulty with this kind of information, accurate as it may be, is that it does not provide any adequate account of the budget circumstances of a university by programs. The university financial complications are presented as one whole, undifferentiated mass. The assumption is that everything the university does is equally important, equally expensive, and equally difficult to finance. The administrator's plea is for more income from whatever source—student fees, endowment, current gifts and grants, and government appropriations—to finance generally everything the university is now doing or may want to do in the future. This is an exceedingly unsophisticated kind of plea. It is probably also an unrealistic plea. It is a plea, however, which is made inevitable by the absence of a planning-programming-budget system within a university.

Already there are indications that far more comprehensive and more exacting methods of budgeting and of information analysis will be needed and indeed will be required on the part of universities in the future than in the past. A technical publication by the American Council on Education has provided guidelines to universities in the development of a planning-programming-budget system.[2] A very detailed and perhaps unduly complicated method of financial analysis has been worked out and proposed for use by colleges and universities.[3] The National Science Foundation has published an out-

2. Harry Williams, *Planning for Effective Resource Allocation in Universities* (Washington: American Council on Education, 1966).

3. John E. Swanson, Wesley Arden, and Homer E. Still, Jr., *Financial Analysis of Current Operations of Colleges and Universities* (Ann Arbor: Institute of Public Administration, University of Michigan, 1966).

line of a comprehensive information program for higher education.[4] All of these proposals provide important and useful procedures for more adequate budgeting and more adequate financial management than many universities have observed in the past.

One more general comment may be appropriate here. If federal government financial assistance is to be extended to higher education more extensively in the future than in the past, then more careful program and program expense data are going to be needed. Otherwise, federal government financial assistance to colleges and universities will produce great inequities in the support provided individual institutions of higher education as a result of differences in programs and in program costs. It is almost an accurate generalization to say that no two colleges and no two universities are ever the same in the activities they perform. Comparisons cannot be made between universities as universities. Valid comparison can only be made between similar programs as undertaken by various universities.

The central concern here is how a systems analysis of a university may contribute to the development of an adequate planning-programming-budget system. I think it is reasonable to assert that there cannot be an adequate planning-programming-budget system within a university without the reinforcement of a systems analysis, and that there cannot be an adequate systems analysis

4. National Science Foundation, *Systems for Measuring and Reporting the Resources and Activities of Colleges and Universities,* NSF 67-15 (Washington: 1967).

without the reinforcement of a planning-programming-budget system. The two are essential to each other.

Earlier we called attention to the fact that one of the peculiar characteristics of a university as an enterprise is the overwhelming importance of its financial operation. A university has certain attributes in common with a governmental administrative agency. A university can undertake to perform with varying degrees of effectiveness only what its financial resources permit. The university has an advantage over an administrative agency of government in that it may draw its financial resources from more varied sources: charges to clients and philanthropic gifts in addition to subventions from the tax resources of government.

In the chart of a systems analysis suggested herein, I have proposed a careful distinction between the capital budget and the operating budget of a university. This distinction is made all the more important, I believe, because the federal government in its program development and appropriation practice does not make this differentiation. Some federal government programs of assistance to higher education are intended to provide only capital facilities, not current operating funds. Moreover, some programs provide loans only (as for student housing), while other programs provide outright grants (as for instructional and research facilities). Programs for student assistance likewise provide loans (to be lent in turn to students) and grants (for work-study, educational opportunity, and graduate fellowships). Whatever the reasons which control federal government program and appropriation practice, it is essential for a university to make a clear distinction between funds providing university capital (such as plant, equipment, and loan funds) and funds providing support for current operations. It is also essential for a university to make a clear distinction between capital funds received as grants and capital funds received as loans. Obviously, the latter receipts must be repaid, usually on an amortization schedule.

The capital plant resources of a university are a vital asset. Such resources must be carefully inventoried, their appropriate use must be assigned, and their effective utilization must be both established and realized. These capital plant resources determine the capacity of the university to perform its various processes and to achieve its desired outputs. Plant facilities have qualitative characteristics as well. They may be good, fair, poor, or obsolete in their adequacy to support the university process. They may be efficient or inefficient in the production of desired outputs.

Presumably, the purpose of a capital budget is to expand university capacity to produce larger outputs, to replace poor or obsolete facilities, and to improve the efficiency of the productive process. Expanded capacity can also be realized by more effective utilization of existing plant. Ordinarily, a capital budget will represent an immediate improvement program and a long-range objective. None of this capital budget is meaningful or purposeful unless it is properly related to the process and the output of a university.

The operating budget of a university represents the allocation of income to the various programs of the university. In reality, much of the income available to a university is earmarked. Endowment income may be available only for student aid, or medical education, or a faculty chair in classical languages. Grant income is practically always earmarked income, usually (in the case of foundation and federal government grants) for research projects. Charges for room and board are obviously intended to be used for the expense of operating residence and dining halls. Thus, much of the income is not general income to be used as the university pleases but to be used as the university has been instructed to do. The allocation of current income often has to be done in terms of particular purposes or activities of a university.

In the systems analysis outlined herein, we have postulated four major processes of a university, with corresponding outputs: student life, instruction, research, and public service. These are broad categories of activity, and within each category there needs to be particular program definitions. Thus, within student life there would be the admissions program, the student aid program, the student health program, the student residence hall program, the student recreation program, the student cultural program (artists and lectures), the student social program, the student publication program (if university financed), the student government program (if university financed), and the intercollegiate athletic program. Within the research category there would be the various separately financed research projects. Within the public service category there would be a variety of programs: the teaching hospital (if owned and operated by a university as an adjunct to medical instruction), agricultural extension, engineering extension or testing, professional institutes and short courses (such as a science teachers' institute), foreign aid projects, and public (general education) broadcasting.

The most important single category of university activity, of course, is instruction. Ordinarily, in most university accounting reports, this instruction category is subdivided into several standard groupings: departmental instruction and research, instructional services (such as audio-visual service, language laboratories, instructional television, etc.), libraries, student services (registration, placement, student counseling, and general service), general expense (publication of catalogues and reports, convocations and commencements, computer center, and public information), operation and maintenance of instructional plant, and general administration. These sub-divisions of instructional activity may be defined in various ways, but such subdivisions are used by most university accounting offices.

I contend that these traditional sub-divisions of reporting the instructional expenditures of universities are almost completely meaningless. These are not program units at all. These sub-divisions of instructional activity are about as helpful as the usual object classification of expenditures: personal services, equipment, supplies, utility services, travel, and other operating expense.

I am not suggesting that universities should abandon either these traditional sub-divisions of instructional expense or the object classification of expenditures. These customary groupings of expenditures have a definite utility, and such coding of accounts is an important element in the accounting practice of a university.

The point here for the purposes of both systems analysis and a planning-programming-budget system is that the instructional activity must be classified first of all by program. Only when there is a standardized set of program classifications within the category of instruction can a university develop a systems analysis and a planning-programming-budget system with any use for academic and financial management. No university in my judgment is utilizing properly the new techniques of programming and systems analysis until it has developed a program classification of its instructional activity.

There can well be a good deal of argument about the most appropriate (and least burdensome) program classification of instruction which might be employed by a university. I offer the following as illustrative but not necessarily definitive:

1. General Education Program
2. Technical Education Program
3. Arts and Sciences Program
   (specialized courses for baccalaureate)
4. Teacher Education Program
   (baccalaureate)
5. Business Administration Program
   (baccalaureate)
6. Engineering Program
   (baccalaureate)

7. Undergraduate Professional Programs
   (agriculture, architecture, art, music, drama, nursing, home economics, pharmacy, journalism)
8. Honors or Tutorial Program
9. Master's Program
10. Graduate-Professional Programs
    (law, dentistry, optometry, veterinary medicine, theology)
11. Doctor of Philosophy Program
12. Doctor of Medicine Program

This classification seems to me to be almost the minimum number of program categories which must be employed within a university in order to develop a clear understanding of expenditure requirements and in order to relate available income to these requirements. It is not enough to develop expenditure data by departments. Expenditure requirements need to be determined by these kinds of instructional programs as such.

The formula for planning budget needs, and incidentally for planning a university's objectives and resource requirements, would be as follows:

a. Faculty Compensation
   1. Number of Students (usually full-time equivalents in terms of credit hours of enrollment)
   2. Average Class Size (faculty load)
   3. Number of Faculty Required
   4. Average Faculty Salary
   5. Average Faculty Fringe Benefit Costs
b. Faculty Support
   1. Personal Services of Assistants, Technicians, and Clerical Personnel
   2. Supplies and Equipment, Travel, Publication
c. Departmental and College Administration
d. Instructional Services (amount per student)

e. Library Services (amount per student)
f. Student Services (amount per student)
g. General Expense (amount per student)
h. Plant Operation (amount per student)
i. General Administration (amount per student)

From these components of expenditure a university could determine what it is spending for each instructional program it offers, what financial resources it has available to defray these expenditure requirements, what changes or improvements it wishes to plan in these expenditure items, how or where the income might be obtained to finance desired improvements, what modifications in items or programs may be necessary because of limitations in available income, and similar issues. Only when a university has these data for its various programs does academic management have the basis for rational decision-making, for systems analysis in financial terms, and for a planning-programming-budget system.

SUMMARY

Systems analysis is a way of examining university activities. Systems analysis looks at university operations in terms of inputs, process, and outputs. Systems analysis seeks to provide an understanding and an information base for decision-making which will permit careful planning, appropriate allocation of resources in terms of desired outputs, and evaluation of effectiveness and efficiency. These are broad goals, and they may have to be approached rather than realized.

At the same time, when higher education is much in the public eye, when greater resources are being sought for university operations, when philanthropist and taxpayer are being asked to contribute more generously to the support of university activities, then university management must avail itself of every possible technique for understanding and clarifying university objectives, processes, and expenditures. Nor is it likely that a university will ever have all the resources which it would like to have to support all the activities it would like to undertake. Under these circumstances, hard choices must be made about inputs, process, and outputs. Such hard choices are likely to be more acceptable to all concerned if they are carefully and rationally made. And it is even possible that in explaining and defining choices, a university will find that additional resources will be forthcoming from those who provide the external sources of university financial support. The American university today can ill afford to do without systems analysis and a planning-programming-budget system.

Financing Higher Education

W hen I undertook to direct the study of the Commission on Financing Higher Education in 1949, the whole subject of the financing of our institutions of higher education in this country was in a state of confusion.[1] It is no exaggeration to say that that state of confusion hasn't changed much in the intervening years. The confusion has become simply more complicated, like everything else.

In 1950 there were several great uncertainties affecting the colleges and universities in the United States. Our institutions of higher education were just emerging from five years of post-war boom, preceded by five years of wartime bust and ten years of depression. In 1947 a Presidential commission had said in effect that a much

1. See report of the Commission on Financing Higher Education, *The Nature and Needs of Higher Education* (New York: Columbia University Press, 1952); and John D. Millett, *Financing Higher Education in the United States* (New York: Columbia University Press, 1952).

larger proportion of all youth ought to go to college, or at least to a community college. In addition, the President's commission said that the federal government should finance the future operations and construction of higher education and that this financial support should be confined to public institutions.[2] Beyond this, the Korean conflict had begun, inflation was mounting again, and there was talk of once more mobilizing the young manpower of the nation (with a corresponding large-scale removal of men students from college and university campuses).

The report of the President's commission was subject to vigorous criticism on three counts. First of all, it was asserted that the large increase in college and university enrollments would result in a lowering of academic standards and that such a proposal was in essence another indication of the anti-intellectual strain in American society. The second criticism was directed to the proposal that the federal government assume the major financial role in the support of public higher education. Since support of public higher education was traditionally a state and local government function, this proposal presupposed a major shift in the pattern of federal-state relationships. Thirdly, it was pointed out that the report of the President's commission in 1947 also presupposed a declining role in American higher education for the

2. Cf. The President's Commission on Higher Education, *Higher Education for American Democracy* (Washington: U.S. Government Printing Office, 1947).

privately sponsored colleges and universities. Here again a traditional pattern was to be abandoned.

The work of the Commission on Financing Higher Education was sponsored by the Association of American Universities under grants from the Rockefeller Foundation and the Carnegie Corporation of New York. The report of the Commission in 1952 was more traditionally oriented than that of the President's commission five years earlier. It called for an increase in all sources of financial support for higher education, and, except in the fields of research and student housing, advocated no enlarged role for the federal government. The two most practical results of the Commission's efforts were the organized activity to expand corporate support of higher education which has been encouraged by the Council on Financial Aid to Education, and the substantial commitment of the Ford Foundation to provide new capital resources to privately sponsored colleges and universities.

Higher education has, of course, greatly increased its enrollment in the past fifteen years. Total enrollment in the autumn of 1950 was just above 2.6 million students. In the autumn of 1967 the enrollment was just under 7 million students. This has meant an increase of two and a half times in a seventeen-year period of time. The financial support of the current operations of higher education has also risen spectacularly in this period. In 1949-50 the current fund income of all institutions of higher education in the United States was reported by the Office of Education to be just about 2.4 billion dollars. By 1959-60 this current fund income had risen to 4.8 billion dollars. The Office of Education estimates that current fund income was 9.6 billion dollars in 1963-64, and I estimate that it was 12.2 billion dollars in 1966-67. If my estimate is approximately correct, our institutions of higher education over a seventeen-year period have increased their current income from 2.4 billion to over 12 billion dollars, which is a 400 percent increase. Thus, a 150 percent increase in enrollment has been accompanied by a fivefold increase in current fund income.

Yet, the financing of higher education in our country is still confused, and still a troublesome problem for everyone concerned about the welfare of higher education in general and about the financing of individual institutions of higher education in particular. There are several reasons for this concern. First of all, the activities of and the expectations from higher education have greatly expanded, and this expansion is not adequately indicated simply by raw data on student enrollment. University research has increased greatly, and now carries the burden of intellectual leadership for all of Western culture. The public service activity of higher education has grown, and still additional burdens are being placed upon it by federal legislation such as the State Technical Services Act of 1965 and Title I of the Higher Education Act of 1965. There is increased emphasis upon graduate education and upon graduate-professional education, and from data I have examined I believe it costs seven or eight times as much to educate a student in medicine or for the Ph.D. degree as it does at the community college level. Secondly, the salaries and the expenses of instruction in higher education have mounted rapidly, and no immediate end to this pressure is in sight. Thirdly, the income support of higher education remains at best uncertain, or remains responsive only within limits to the increased instructional and other demands placed upon higher education.

I cannot undertake here a careful or detailed historical or current analytical report on financing higher education. There is a need for such a report, since we have not had a full-scale study of this subject since 1952. But our most urgent need, I submit, is for an adequate, informative framework within which to analyze the financial requirements and the financial resources of our system of higher education. We do not have such a framework at this time, and a great part of the present confusion about the financing of higher education can be traced to this single situation.

In a simplified form, I propose to set forth here my concept of what is needed today as a framework for analysis and discussion of higher education financing. I shall illustrate the importance of this framework by use of estimated expenditure and income data on the current operations of higher education for the academic or fiscal year 1966-67. Necessarily, these estimates are at the best educated guesses based upon recent trends. Moreover, by expressing these estimates in terms of billions of dollars only, there are many refinements and details which are glossed over. These details are not unimportant, but they are of secondary interest in my effort to suggest general circumstances.

There are at least five different elements or factors to be considered in any careful analysis of the financing of higher education. These elements are: (1) activities, (2) sources of income, (3) application of funds, (4) types of instructional programs, and (5) sponsorship of institutions. Each of these will be discussed in turn. It is important at the outset, however, to make a few general observations.

First of all, it should be borne in mind that analysis of the financial condition of higher education is essentially an analysis of individual and separate schools, colleges, and universities. Every institution is peculiar in terms of enrollment size, physical location, student clientele, instructional programs offered, and other characteristics. These peculiarities make comparisons hazardous, generalizations faulty, and actual difficulties uncertain.

Secondly, it seems evident that fiscal management in many institutions of higher education is in a rudimentary stage of development. I make this generalization with full awareness that it will appear to be highly critical of administrative competence in our colleges and universities. I am not suggesting that administrators do not know where the money comes from or how it is used. Financial records are quite detailed. The fault lies in the frequent failure to use adequate tools of fiscal analysis: to employ program concepts, to weigh alternative use of funds, and to employ some kind of benefit analysis or marginal utility analysis in the allocation of funds. Undoubtedly, much more sophisticated fiscal management is going to be needed in the future than in the past.

ACTIVITIES

It is customary to present the purposes or objectives of higher education as threefold: instruction, research, and public service. Surely these three purposes are sufficiently important to be utilized as the major designations of higher education activity for financial reporting and fiscal management.

To these three principal kinds of activity two more must be added: auxiliary *services* and student aid. I much prefer the designation of auxiliary services to that of auxiliary enterprises for obvious reasons. We in higher education need to avoid the implication that we are engaged in business-type acitvities. This is desirable both from the standpoint of public relations and from the standpoint of possible difficulty with the Internal Revenue Service.

There are some faculty objections to making a financial distinction between instruction and research, and these objections are understandable. Yet, the facts of life are that large-scale research requiring extensive facilities, equipment, supplies, and personnel (either part-time or full-time) is going to be financed primarily by the federal government. Moreover, such research is by the nature of things going to be performed primarily by universities (I include Massachusetts Institute of Technology and California Institute of Technology in this category, as does the Association of American Universities). I hope individual faculty members will continue to have the opportunity to engage in their own personal research activity, and the financial cost of this opportunity should properly be included in the category of instructional expense. We distort the financial realities of our higher education operations, however, when we do not clearly separate instruction from sponsored research.

For example, federal government financial support is almost completely lacking for the instruction activity of higher education. The federal government underwrites the instructional expense of certain federally sponsored colleges and universities, such as the military academies and Howard University. The federal government distributes a modest amount of annual operating funds under the Morrill Act of 1890, as amended, to the land-grant colleges and universities established under the Morrill Act of 1862. The federal government also provides a modest amount of instructional assistance to those universities receiving fellowship funds under Title IV of the National Defense Education Act. In general, these are the major federal funds available for instructional purposes. My guess is that these came in total to about 200 million dollars in 1966-67, while federal government support of research was over 2 billion dollars that year. It is facts of this nature which are concealed by the present financial reporting practices of American higher education.

A word may be added about public service, because I suspect that this is going to become an even more important category of federal expenditure in the near future. There are various definitions of what a category of expenditure and income labeled "public service" ought to include, but I would argue that it should encompass continuing education (including institutes for elementary and secondary school teachers, agricultural extension, outlays under Title I of the Higher Education Act of 1965, and general television activities), the operation of teaching hospitals, activities on behalf of the Agency for International Development, and activities for the Peace Corps and the Office of Economic Opportunity. These are all important undertakings, but support of these endeavors is not the same as support of the instruction activity of higher education.

I estimate the total expenditures of higher education in 1966-67 for current operations were divided by major activities approximately as follows (in billions of dollars):

Instruction	6.0
Research	2.5
Public Service	1.0
Auxiliary Service	2.0
Student Aid	0.5
	12.0

INCOME

There are three known ways of financing the expenditure needs of higher education in the United States. These are: (1) charges, (2) government, and (3) philanthropy. All play an important part in making the operations of higher education possible.

In 1966-67 my estimate is that higher education received its current operating income from these sources (in billions of dollars):

Charges		5.0
Government		6.2
State	3.0	
Federal	2.9	
Local	0.3	
Philanthropy		1.0
Endowment	0.4	
Gifts	0.6	
		——
		12.2

It is customary for higher education current fund income to exceed current fund expenditures in any one year. The federal government under the college housing loan program, for example, requires that there be a surplus of income over expenditure in the operation of residence halls and student conters. The same is true of private indentures written to cover the borrowing of funds with which to construct residence halls. In any event, the surplus income usually goes into student aid or into capital accounts (reserves and working capital, construction of new plant, and additional endowment).

The category of charges includes more than student tuition or instructional fees. This income also embraces charges to students for room and board, charges for food service at a student center facility, charges for admission to intercollegiate athletic events, sales at bookstores, rent collected from college or university owned housing, and similar income.

Government necessarily means not just the federal government but state and local governments as well. It is my best guess that in the year ending June 30, 1967, state and local government support of higher education still exceeded federal government support, but there is little question but that federal government financial assistance to the current operations of higher education is rapidly increasing and may soon exceed the combined total of state and local support.

Philanthropy is of two kinds: endowment income and gifts and bequests received for current operations or additions to capital. Such philanthropic support may come from private foundations, business corporations, alumni, friends, church groups, and voluntary associations.

A good deal of attention is continually given to the matter of increasing the income of higher education received from these three sources of support. Charges to students, especially tuition and instructional fees, have been on the increase, and proposals for deduction of these fees from income taxes are intended to help make these increases easier for various families to pay, especially families in the higher brackets of federal income taxation. Government increases in support must be sought through the executive and legislative budget process. This inevitably means increased taxation or increased deficit spending, and both encounter substantial public resistance. Much of federal government support to higher education is geared to defense and international aid spending, and is likely to suffer the varied public and administrative fortunes of these activities. Philanthropy depends upon the giving mood of foundation executives, corporation executives, church groups, and individuals of varying degree of affluence. There seems to be no single, simple solution to the search for means of augmenting these three sources of higher education support.

ARTICULATION
OF INCOME AND ACTIVITY

The data on gross distribution of expenditures by major activity and by principal sources of income are not very meaningful. It is essential to take the additional step of articulating income support to the separate activities of institutions of higher education.

There are two ways of looking at the current fund income of colleges and universities. One way is to consider all current income as a pool from which to defray the expense of any activity as needed. The other way is to look at all or much of current fund income as earmarked to support particular activities, or even particular undertakings and projects within a category of major activity. Individual colleges and universities receive both kinds of income, but I believe earmarked income now exceeds pooled or general income, and that it is time for accounting systems and financial reports clearly to reflect this condition.

It is very difficult from available financial data to make reasonable estimates of the articulation of higher education income with major activities. I have endeavored to make estimates upon the basis of such guidelines as are available.

Properly, we should begin with the category of instruction, or of "instruction and general operation" as I would prefer to designate this category. Table I shows

TABLE 1

Estimated Current Expenditure and Income
For Instruction
1966-67
(In Billions of Dollars)

Expenditure		Income		
1. Departmental		1. Charges		2.5
Instruction	3.6	2. Government		3.0
2. Libraries	0.4	a. State	2.5	
3. Plant Operation	1.0	b. Federal	0.2	
4. Administration		c. Local	0.3	
and General	1.0	3. Philanthropy		0.8
		a. Endowments	0.3	
		b. Gifts	0.5	
	6.0			6.3

in billions of dollars the estimated expenditure of higher education for instruction and general activity in 1966-67. There are many comments which might be made about these data. Two observations will suffice. Student charges fall substantially short of providing the income needed for the instructional activity of higher education, and insofar as government support of higher education is concerned, it is state government support which is crucial to the instructional operation of higher education in the United States.

This last circumstance is exactly reversed, however, when we examine the expenditure and income accounts for the research activity of higher education. Here federal government support is the critical factor, as shown in Table 2. The excess of research income over direct research expenditure is used to defray plant operation and administrative overhead of individual institutions.

In Table 3 we may observe the expenditure and in-

TABLE 2

Estimated Current Expenditure and Income
For Research
1966-67
(In Billions of Dollars)

Expenditure		*Income*		
1. Sponsored Research	2.5	1. Government		2.5
		a. Federal	2.2	
		b. State	0.3	
		2. Philanthropy		0.1
				2.6

come pattern for public service. At best these data are approximations, and ideally it ought to be possible to take each sub-category of activity and relate to it each category of income. This is impossible under present reporting. We know in general that medical centers are supported by patient charges (including insurance and

TABLE 3
Estimated Current Expenditures and Income
For Public Service, Auxiliary Service,
and Student Aid
1966-67
(In Billions of Dollars)

Expenditures		Income		
PUBLIC SERVICE				
1. Medical Centers	0.4	1. Charges		0.5
2. Continuing Education	0.3	2. Government		0.5
3. International	0.2	a. Federal	0.3	
4. Other	0.1	b. State	0.2	
	1.0			1.0
AUXILIARY SERVICE				
1. Residence Halls	1.5	1. Charges		2.0
2. Student Unions	0.2			
3. Athletics	0.2			
4. Other	0.1			
	2.0			
STUDENT AID				
1. Total	0.5	1. Government		0.2
		a. Federal	0.2	
		2. Philanthropy		0.1
				0.3

welfare payments) and by state government appropriations. The agricultural extension service is supported by federal and state government funds, while other continuing education activity tends to be supported by student charges, with the federal government just now beginning to enter this field. University projects overseas are supported almost entirely by federal funds.

Auxiliary services tend to be supported entirely by charges, although in many individual instances intercollegiate athletics requires a subsidy from the general account of the college or university. I show a balance of income and expenditure in this activity category, but this conceals a surplus of income for residence halls and a subsidy for student centers and athletics at many individual institutions.

Student aid—and I exclude student loan operations from this category as a capital rather than a current fund transaction—includes only the scholarship, fellowship, and other grants made through college and university channels. These include fellowship funds provided by the federal government and other sutdent aid funds given to institutions by the federal government, with the institutions free to select the individual recipient. In future years, educational opportunity grants will appear in this category of financial activity. I do not include state scholarship funds here, however, since these awards are made directly to individual students and not to institutions.

Student aid awards usually exceed in amount the income earmarked for this purpose. As a result, general income which might otherwise be available for instruction must be used to support student aid. It will be interesting to see whether this situation will continue under the impact of new student aid funds provided by government. It would be helpful, also, if our financial reports could reflect actual waivers or reduction in stated instructional fees which are granted to students by many institutions.

In general, the financial structure of higher education suggests these primary observations:

1. Sponsored research activity will tend to vary as funds are available, and the volume will depend upon how much the federal government will appropriate for this purpose and upon how much the institutions of higher education can undertake to perform effectively.

2. The public service activity generally depends upon avaliable funds from government and from student charges. This activity can and will be expanded or contracted as funds are provided. The support of teaching hospitals needed in conjunction with medical instruction and instruction in other health professions remains a major expenditure problem.

3. Auxiliary services tend to be self-supporting from charges, although for some institutions intercollegiate athletics is not self-supporting.

4. Student aid is an expression of institutional endeavor to recruit good students as well as to encourage students to enter college or to undertake graduate study. The volume of this activity reflects institutional efforts from available funds to build up the quality of their instruction, to build up their enrollment, and to assist needy students.

5. The critical problem of higher educational finance is finding the needed support for instructional activity.

CURRENT
VERSUS CAPITAL ACCOUNT

Obviously, institutions of higher education must have capital plant facilities with which to carry out their activities. Unfortunately, we have very little information about capital plant financing for higher education. In general, we know that instructional plant depends upon philanthropic giving and government appropriations. The federal government has now entered this picture on a large-scale basis through the Higher Education Facilities Act of 1963. Research plant has been provided 100 percent by the federal government in some instances and on a 50 percent basis in other instances. Public service plant—such as continuing education centers—has been provided from private foundation gifts and borrowed funds. Medical centers are now being expanded with substantial assistance from the federal government. Residence hall plant and student center plant are usually built from borrowed funds, with the federal government under the College Housing Loan Program a major supplier of this capital. But this is a *loan,* not a grant program.

In addition to capital plant facilities, colleges and universities have endowment funds to manage, and today they even have good opportunities to invest working capital funds. Student loan funds represent a capital transaction, since they involve the loaning of capital which is to be repaid at a future data with interest on the assistance provided.

In all discussions of higher education finance, it is very important to observe the distinction between current operations and the capital account of an institution. Many gifts and many government appropriations are earmarked for the capital account, not for the current account. Moreover, many federal government programs of financial assistance to institutions of higher education—the housing program, Title II of the National Defense Education Act, Title III of the Higher Education Facilities Act of 1963—are capital assistance programs and not current operations assistance programs. In addition, in the instances just mentioned, these programs are loan and not capital gift programs.

In 1959-60 the Office of Education reported that institutions of higher education invested 1.3 billion dollars in capital plant facilities. These data were not published until 1964.[3] Plant fund income is reported to have come from these sources (in billions of dollars):

Borrowing	0.4
State Government	0.3
Philanthropy	0.2
Current Funds	0.3
Federal Government	0.1
	1.3

3. *Financial Statistics of Institutions of Higher Education,* 1959-60, Office of Education—50023-60, Circular No. 744 (Washington: U.S. Government Printing Office, 1964).

It is not possible from available data to determine the object of such investments by major categories of higher education activity.

In 1965 the Office of Education published an inventory of college and university facilities, but the data were as of December 31, 1957.[4] This report showed 41,000 buildings in use. By type of activity these buildings were divided approximately as follows:

Instruction	11,800
Research	2,600
Residential	20,200
Auxiliary	1,800
General	4,600

The general category included student health facilities, chapels, heating and power plants, maintenance shops, storage facilities, non-teaching hospitals, and staff office buildings.

It seems apparent that there is much still to be done in reporting and analyzing capital plant financing for higher education. The federal government does not make a distinction between capital appropriations and appropriations for current operations. As a result, reports about federal support of higher education provide figures on a fiscal year basis but often fail to indicate how much of this support was for buildings or loan funds and how

4. *College and University Facilities Survey,* Part 3, Inventory of College and University Physical Facilities, Office of Education—51007 (Washington: U.S. Government Printing Office, 1965)

much was for such current operations as instruction, research, public service, and student aid.[5]

Institutions of higher education cannot afford this luxury of failing to distinguish between their current accounts and their capital accounts. Income of each institution must be carefully segregated in terms of current and capital application and accounted for separately in the current operating statements and the statement of assets and liabilities.

INSTRUCTIONAL PROGRAMS

Institutions of higher education tend to be organized upon the basis of departments set up according to scholarly disciplines or professional fields of study. The instructional budget usually contains a single broad category of expense which is labeled "departmental instruction and research." The difficulty with this practice is that it does not recognize a program differentiation in instructional activity.

It is part of the current conventional wisdom of higher education that upper division courses cost more to provide than lower division courses, that doctoral degree students are more expensive to instruct than master's degree students, that medical education costs more than legal education at the graduate-professional level, that graduate

5. Cf. National Science Foundation, *Federal Support to Universities and Colleges*, Fiscal Years 1963-66, NSF 67-14 (Washington, D. C.: U.S. Government Printing Office, 1967).

instruction in physics is more expensive than graduate instruction in teacher education. The difficulty is that few institutions have ever undertaken to cost these differences.

Moreover, universities tend to engage in a wide variety of instructional programs and to undertake more research than a separate liberal arts college. The cost experience of a separate graduate-professional school of theology may be expected to be quite different from the cost experience of a graduate-professional school of law. The cost experience of a community college offering only lower division courses may be expected to be quite different from the cost experience of a four-year college.

Unfortunately, there are almost no nation-wide data to permit us to make a program analysis of instructional expenditures. A good deal of such data is being collected by state-wide boards of higher education or the state-sponsored colleges and universities of each state. It is not clear whether or not these data are comparable from one state to another. We may find some hint at the differences in expense and income patterns of institutions by program from an examination of the financing of types of institutions. This procedure offers only a hint, however. The need is for a definite procedure of program analysis of expense and income.

The diversity of our institutions of higher education is a well-known characteristic. In its classification of institutions for the 1966-67 *Education Directory* (Part 3), the Office of Education employs a twofold classification insofar as instructional offerings are concerned. One is an eleven-fold classification by "type of program," ranging from "terminal-occupational" (presumably meaning technical education) to that of a liberal arts and general program with three or more professional schools. In addition, there is a fivefold classification by "level of offering," ranging from "2 to 4 years" beyond the high school to the doctor of Philosophy degree. Actually, this is a four-fold grouping, since the fifth category, labeled "other" seems to have little meaning or purpose.

The instructional programs of higher education do need to be identified both by type and by level. It would seem useful, however, to employ somewhat fewer and more clearly differentiated categories than those utilized in recent years by the Office of Education.

SPONSORSHIP

In addition to variations in types of instructional program, institutions of higher education differ from one another in terms of sponsorship, that is, in terms of the groups or governments which have established these institutions and which presumably assume some continuing obligation to assist their operation. Sponsorship may influence or affect the financing of various institutions.

The two familiar categories of sponsorship are public and private. These categories in and of themselves do not tell us very much. Public sponsorship must be subdivided into federal, state, and local. Private sponsorship must be sub-divided into non-sectarian and church-related. A state university depends in large part upon a state government to finance its instructional programs. A church-related college or theological seminary depends in some part (to a lesser or greater degree) upon a church body to help finance its instructional program. In any event, the factor of sponsorship is an important conditioning circumstance which needs to be examined carefully in evaluating the financial record of individual colleges and universities.

Table 4 is an approximation of the number of non-profit institutions of higher education in the United States as of 1966-67 by four types and by five kinds of sponsorship. Universities are institutions offering degrees at the Doctor of Philosophy level. In general, colleges are institutions providing an undergraduate education to the baccalaureate level. This category includes the five service academies of the federal government. Professional schools are of varied type: engineering schools, music conservatories, teachers colleges, art institutes, and theological seminaries. The programs of this group as a whole are quite varied; their common characteristic is their tendency to concentrate upon a single kind of professional preparation. Finally, the community colleges offer as a rule two years of technical education and two years of college transfer courses.

As I have indicated earlier, any comparisons of cost experience among various kinds of institutions must be made in terms of instructional programs and other activ-

TABLE 4
Number of Institutions of Higher Education
By Type and Sponsorship
1966-67

	Univer-sities	Colleges	Profes-sional Schools	Commu-nity Colleges	Total
PUBLIC					
Federal	1	5	4	1	11
State	106	87	180	61	434
Local	5	3	7	346	361
PRIVATE					
Non-Sectarian	74	210	127	90	501
Church-Related	49	518	179	160	906
Total	235	823	497	658	2,213

Source: Office of Education, *Education Directory, 1966-1967,* Part 3, "Higher Education" (U.S. Government Printing Office, 1967), Tables 4 and 5. I have ommitted proprietary institutions, and have included "other" as professional schools.

ities if these comparisons are to have any meaning. The labels of various kinds of institutions are at best only a general indication of the kinds of instructional programs and other activities in which they may engage. There are differences of circumstance as well. A community college or even a university serving a metropolitan area would be expected to spend very little on the housing and feeding of students. A theology seminary would be expected to collect very little if anything from student charges. These are but illustrations of the kinds of differences in financing which arise between different kinds of institutions.

The data presented in Table 5 are intended to be illustrative of varying financial characteristics of different types of institutions providing different kinds of instructional programs and conducting different kinds of activities. It must be emphasized that these estimates of expenditure and income refer to *current* operations and are not intended to include any capital funds. It must also be noted that available data do not permit any attempt to integrate income with the five major activities of higher education.

With all these limitations—and the data are even more sketchy and inadequate than I have explained—it is still possible to point to certain special aspects of the financing problems which confront higher education in the United States. First, the category of public university is primarily comprised of state universities. The state funds provided these institutions are devoted primarily to instruction. The federal government funds provided state universities are primarily devoted to research activity, although some of these funds may be earmarked for public service (agricultural extension) and for student aid.

Private universities receive federal funds for research and for student aid. They have enrollments which are only about one-third those of the public universities.[6]

6. Garland Parker in his classification and enrollment data showed a grand total of over 2 million students in public universities in

TABLE 5
Estimated Current Expenditure and Income
By Types of Institutions
1966-67
(In Billions of Dollars)

Expenditures		*Income*		
A. UNIVERSITIES—PUBLIC				
1. Instructions	2.0	1. Charges		1.6
2. Research	1.2	2. Government		3.1
3. Public Service	0.7	a. Federal	1.2	
4. Auxiliary Service	0.7	b. State	1.8	
5. Student Aid	0.1	c. Local	0.1	
		3. Philanthropy		0.1
	4.7			4.8
B. UNIVERSITIES—PRIVATE				
1. Instruction	1.0	1. Charges		0.9
2. Research	0.8	2. Government		1.0
3. Public Service	0.2	a. Federal	1.0	
4. Auxiliary Service	0.3	3. Philanthropy		0.7
5. Student Aid	0.2			
	2.5			2.6
C. COLLEGES—PRIVATE				
1. Instruction	0.8	1. Charges		0.9
2. Auxiliary Service	0.3	2. Philanthropy		0.3
3. Student Aid	0.1			
	1.2			1.2

the autumn of 1966 as against 692,000 students in private universities. See Garland G. Parker, "Statistics of Attendance in American Universities and Colleges, 1966-67," *School and Society* (Vol. 95), January 7, 1967, pp. 11, 12.

TABLE 5 *(Continued)*

D. COMMUNITY COLLEGES—PUBLIC

1. Instruction	0.4	1. Charges		0.1
		2. Government		0.3
		a. Local	0.2	
		b. State	0.1	
	0.4			0.4

These private universities probably spend twice as much for student aid as public universities, in spite of the disparity in enrollments. It is probably safe to say that private universities would carry on no sponsored, and no *large-scale,* research without federal government support.

Private colleges perform very little research and so receive from the federal government only support for student aid. The data were too uncertain to permit any estimate of what this amount might have been in 1966-67. Private colleges must depend upon philanthropy in order to balance their expenditures for instruction and student aid. Presumably, they do balance their expenditure for auxiliary services with their charges to students for this activity.

In the case of community colleges, there is almost a complete concentration upon instruction insofar as activities are concerned, and available income from student charges, local tax support, and state government subvention must meet this need.

The omission of certain categories of expenditure and income does not mean that there are no such expenditures or income but only that the amounts involved are too small to show up in a table where the minimum figure represents 100 million dollars of outlay. The differences are quite obvious and require no special comment, other than to observe the heavy federal government support to private universities and the relative absence of any federal government assistance to private colleges or to public community colleges.

CONCLUSION

I have sought in this paper to provide a framework for the analysis of the financial problems of higher education and at the same time to suggest something about the general magnitude of current and capital outlays for higher education.

The real problems of financing higher education occur, however, at the level of the individual institution: the particular college, professional school, or university. It is the aggregate of all these separate problems and their separate solutions which determine the general welfare and the general affluence of higher education.

At the same time, as government becomes more prominent in the financing of higher education, cooperative action and central planning will probably also become more evident in seeking solutions to the financial needs of individual institutions of higher education.

The Structure of Communications in a University

I am intrigued by the far-reaching implication of these two words "structure" and "communication." I construe "structure" in this particular context to be synonymous with the word "organization," and I construe "communications" to refer not just to mechanics of transmission but to the substance of educational policy. Obviously, in such light one is invited to consider almost any and all phases of the university which may strike his fancy.

Organization means an organic whole with differentiated parts. Organization is people working together for a common objective. Organization is the structure of an enterprise, and in our concern here that enterprise is a university. But enterprises operate in a larger context; they are subject to the external influences and constraints of the social institution of which they are a part and of the society in which they exist. This means that the

An Address for the Twenty-First Annual National Summer Conference for Academic Deans, Stillwater, Oklahoma July 31, 1967 organization of any particular university is responsive to its role in the broader sphere of the institution of higher education and of a democratic society.

Communication in its fullest sense means shared understanding of a shared purpose. Only in an organizational setting is such communication essential, since primarily it is different groups of persons performing different tasks in an enterprise who are in need of a shared understanding of a shared purpose. Communication presupposes a common purpose, and it sets as its objective the realization of a common understanding of that goal which an enterprise exists to achieve.

It is always difficult to know where to begin in a discussion of organizational structure. Should one start with social setting and institutional context? Should one start with a particular enterprise? Should one start with abstractions of experience drawn from several individual enterprises? These are not easy questions to answer; wherever one begins he is likely to move back and forth from one level of experience and operation to another. If this is not the case, then one may well be criticized for presenting only a partial account of a complicated phenomenon.

There is, however, one limitation to our subject matter. We are not so much concerned with structure in and of itself as we are with structure for communication within a university. I take this to be an important, indeed vital, qualification. We are saying in effect, I believe, that we seek a structure of specialization within a university which will facilitate communication. We are saying in effect that within the university there can be a shared understanding of a shared purpose. Our inquiry then is directed to the question of how can structure contribute to understanding.

I begin this inquiry with a generalization which may appear to be a truism but which unfortunately is not commonly accepted by students of organization and which is often not understood by persons outside the field of higher education. A university is a unique enterprise. I think this uniqueness may perhaps best be illustrated if we take a systems approach to the analysis of a university.

In any systems analysis there are three major elements: the input factors, the technology or process of operation, and the output. In an industrial enterprise, for example, the inputs are raw materials, labor, management, and capital (including land, plant, and equipment), the technology is a particular manufacturing process, and the output is one or more finished items or goods produced by the enterprise.

In a university the inputs are knowledge as represented by a faculty, students, research ideas, and capital (including land, plant, and equipment). The technology is made up of an instructional process and a research process. The output comprises graduated students, other students, and advancements in knowledge. What strikes one immediately and forcefully about such an analysis of higher education is the indefinite quality of the entire system. Among the input factors, only capital in the form of land, buildings, and equipment can be defined with some precision. Capital in the form of knowledge and in the form of faculty talent is certainly an elusive factor. Research ideas or projects as the basis for the research process may be written down but the generation of such ideas is again an uncertain element. Students, both regular and short-term, are presumably motivated to acquire and use knowledge, but their ability and interest to do so are not simple to ascertain.

Similarly, when we turn to the technology of higher education we are impressed by the highly uncertain features of both the instructional process and the research process. For degree purposes the instructional process is usually highly structured in terms of a formal curriculum with course units and credit hour requirements. The satisfactory completion of these courses and the accumulation of the required credit hours produces a graduated student. This student has presumably acquired the knowledge necessary for continued learning, and such skill as may be necessary for the use of this knowledge, the teaching of this knowledge, and the advancement of this knowledge. But much of the instructional process also involves what we often term public service, such as the continuing or adult education of various persons for non-degree purposes and the application of knowledge to special problems through consulting services or through actual application as in a teaching hospital. Moreover, the research process will presumably produce new knowledge, but the result or the importance of the results are by no means assured.

The outputs of the university are graduated students. other instructed students, new knowledge, and sometimes advice about the actual application of knowledge to specific problems. To be sure, we can count the number of degrees granted and the number of persons enrolled in short courses. We cannot be certain about the quality or usefulness of those student products of our instructional process. We can list research publications. We cannot be certain about the actual extent to which new knowledge has actually been provided or about the actual utility of any of this new knowledge.

In addition to all these indefinite characteristics of the university system, note another pecularity. Economic analysis of the business firm has always accorded a major role to the entrepreneur and more recently to business management. Where in a university system do we acknowledge a role for management of the instructional and research process? I purposefully do not enumerate management as an input factor in the university system. I do not do so for a very important reason. Management in a university is essential, I believe, even as is management in a business enterprise. But the role of management is quite different. In a business enterprise management must assure that the input factors are processed in such a way with the appropriate technology to produce the intended products, such as an automobile, a machine tool, a television set, or a high-rise office building. In the university enterprise management must assure an appropriate environment for learning and research but management cannot control the technology in such a way as to assure the desired end product. The technology is too personal, too individualized, too uncertain for strict control. Indeed, strict control may impair rather than facilitate the realization of that environment of learning which does result in an output of learned students and of new knowledge.

The internal organization structure of a university should not be confused with the internal organization structure of other types of enterprises with very different input factors, a very different technology, and a very different output or end purpose.

The essential concern remains to be examined: the particular structure of the university. There are, I believe, two primary determinants of structure in most enterprises. One of these is the state of technology in the process of the enterprise and the other is the end product sought to be produced, that is, the desired output. The art of organization consists in large part of evaluating the respective impact of process and output upon an enterprise and of devising a structure which will integrate the two.

When we look at the technology of higher education, we must begin necessarily with the prevailing practice which obtains in the division of labor, or in the specialization of work. I think it is quite clear that specialization in the field of higher education is by the subject-matter content of knowledge. There may have been a time—I'm doubtful about this—one hundred years or more ago in Western culture when there was very little specialization in the content of knowledge. Professors and tutors may then have believed that there was a single, unified body of knowledge which students could acquire and which then became the mark of an educated man. If such an idea were operative a century or more ago, it is obviously not effective today. The great increase in knowledge has been made possible in large part because of specialized inquiries into particular parts or subjects, and the scope of knowledge is so great that expertise can be realized only in one field or indeed one sub-field.

The university as an enterprise recognizes first of all specialization of faculty effort in instruction and research by particular fields of knowledge. These specializations are divided into two major categories, the disciplines and the professional fields; into four groupings of disciplines (the humanities, the social sciences, the biological sciences, and the physical sciences and mathematics), and into various professions (art, architecture, agricultural science and management, engineering, teacher education, business operation and management, music, law, medicine, theology, home economics, drama, dentistry, veterinary medicine, pharmacy, optometry, social work, public administration, etc.); and into separate departments in the disciplines (history, economics, botany, and physics, for example), and into specializations of professions (such as painting, landscape architecture, internal medicine, criminal law, school administration, accountancy, and agricultural economics).

In other words, the technology of higher education is based upon specialization in the content of knowledge. This specialization is growing apace. There are, to be sure, inter-disciplinary and inter-professional endeavors which seek to focus several specializations upon a particular problem. Molecular biology is a spectacular illustration of a combination of physical science, biological science, and medicine upon one part of the organic process of life. The disciplines of philosophy, government, economics, sociology, anthropology, and history must be combined in the professional education of law. A project in the exploration of space is an endeavor requiring a combination of the physical sciences and mathematics, the biological sciences, the social sciences, engineering, business management, and public administration. Knowledge about an area of the world such as Africa demands mastery of such disciplines as anthropology, geography, economics, history, and government.

Regardless of the inter-disciplinary nature of various professions, various projects, and various problems of study, it remains clear that the basic specialization of university activity for instruction and research is by disciplines and by professional fields. This kind of specialization may be criticized as unduly narrow, as artificial and unrealistic, even as chauvinistic on occasion, but the fact is still evident that the specialization of departments by disciplines and by professional subjects is the viable, enduring specialization within the university process.

I see no reasonable alternative in the technology of higher education other than the department as the basic unit of organizational structure. This is the basic unit with which most of us are familiar from our education and from our own participation in a higher education enterprise. This is the basic unit which gives the greatest promise of providing creative leadership and individual performance in producing the desired outputs of higher education. This is the basic unit which in spite of all its acknowledged deficiencies continues to be recognized as essential to the higher education process.

Specialization of work is not the only consideration to be given attention in establishing and perpetuating a structure for a university. A second determinant is the product or output of the higher education process. As I have already indicated, this output has at least four items or four different objectives: the graduated student, the re-educated student, applied service (often labeled "public" service), and research results. How do these desired end products affect the structure of a university? The answer is, of course, that they affect the structure in several different ways.

For one thing, the graduated student may be produced at several different levels of formal education or of educational intensity. These levels are as follows:

1. The two-year program, or associate degree level.
2. The four-year program, or baccalaureate level in arts and sciences.
3. The four- or five-year program or baccalaureate level in a professional field of study.

4. The master's degree level in arts and sciences or in a professional field of study.

5. The doctor's degree level in arts and sciences or in a professional field of study.

6. The graduate-professional degree program in law, medicine, dentistry, theology, or similar profession.

If the basic operating unit of a university is accepted as a department, then each department must be prepared to contribute its appropriate effort to the production of these various outputs in terms of graduated students. Not every department, to be sure, will necessarily be involved in instructional activity at all six levels of student output. It will not be unusual, however, for a department to have as many as four of these outputs for its instructional process, and I can think of individual instances in which a department might very well be involved in five levels of output.

But the graduated student—the degree-receiving student—is only one kind of end product of the university. We must also have a university structure which produces the re-educated or the continually educated student, the applied service, and the research result. These additional end products must be provided from university technology, or these objectives must be disassociated from the enterprise of a university.

My own belief is that the department structure of a university in varying proportions may be expected to embrace these additional end purposes or outputs. Not all of these outputs will be a part of the objectives of every university, and not every department will be involved with equal intensity in the pursuit of these additional outputs. To some extent I suspect that every department in a university will find itself engaged in the process of producing some outputs in re-educated students, in applied service, and in research.

For budgetary, for staffing, or for other sufficient reasons, a department or a university may decide that these additional outputs need some special structural identification in order to ensure their realization. Unfortunately, we employ such a wide range of labels within our various universities that there is no such thing as a common designation for these structural practices. I wish we could develop some kind of standard nomenclature for university structure. In the absence of this, I think each individual university might well strive for structural clarity and precision by establishing a standard nomenclature for internal use.

I suggest that the word "institute" or "laboratory" be restricted to use in identifying specialized research units in a university. I think the label "center" might be used to identify inter-disciplinary instructional units, although the designation "school" might be equally employed for this purpose. I believe the word "service" might be utilized to identify programs or activities involving re-education and consulting assistance. But regardless of any particular set of terminological labels, I urge that any one university should observe some consistency in its practice of establishing units of operation to supplement the basic structure of departments.

It may be noted in passing that there is a good deal of interest today in what is variously labeled "project" organization or "task force" organization. Essentially, these are concepts of a special problem-solving effort which will usually be of limited duration in time. The management of an enterprise may decide that the regular or prevailing organization is not well adapted to produce some immediate purpose or product. The various operating units of the organization, the various supervisory units, and the various top-management units may then be directed to provide personnel to staff a project or task-force endeavor of the enterprise. As a "crash" or special purpose structural arrangement, this organizational device has many advantages. Presumably, the arrangement is only a short-term one. Otherwise, I think we may assume that the basic organizational pattern of the whole enterprise is poorly adapted to desired outputs and to the required production processes.

Thus far I have discussed the basic organizational structure of a university; that is, the basic operating units of a university. I have suggested that both in terms of process and output we must consider the academic department as the basic operating unit, even though there are various levels of output in graduated students and even though there are other additional outputs to be realized. I have suggested also that particular special purpose units may be established, such as research institutes, area study centers, and hospital service or broadcasting service. Even where these additional units are employed, I think it highly desirable that assigned personnel still have a firm commitment also to a particular academic department.

In discussing the organizational structure of an enterprise such as a university, it is not sufficient, however, to confine our attention to the basic operating units. In any enterprise, we will also find as indispensable elements a structure of coordination and a structure of management. Time will not permit me here to provide an adequate statement of general organizational theory upon which I base this assertion. I must take the practice as demonstrated from experience and the theory as empirically proven.

In a university the structure of coordination consists of colleges and faculties. Complications arise when we do not clearly differentiate between the two different aspects of coordination. Personally, I believe we should employ the term "college" to indicate arrangements for supervising and coordinating the instructional programs of a university. For two-year programs we might well have a General College. For a baccalaureate program we need a College of Arts and Sciences and Colleges of Business Administration, Education, Engineering, Agriculture, Nursing, and similar units. At the graduate level we need a Graduate College. At the graduate-professional level we need Colleges of Medicine, Law, Dentistry, and other appropriate units.

We should understand that colleges are arrangements for coordinating the activities of departments in the output of graduated students. Thus, the concerns of colleges should properly embrace standards of admission for students, degree requirements, curriculum offerings and course structure, student counseling, evaluation of student academic performance, and instructional procedures. Colleges need to concentrate their attention upon the process whereby student imputs are converted into the output of degree-receiving students. Colleges exist to supervise and accomplish the various instructional programs which a university decides it is appropriate and necessary for it to undertake.

There is a second structure of coordination needed in a university which for lack of a better term we shall designate faculty affairs. By faculty matters I mean standards of initial appointment of members in a department, standards of faculty rank, standards of faculty promotion, standards of faculty compensation, evaluation of faculty performance, standards of faculty work loads in various instructional programs, faculty research policies, faculty outside-consulting policies, and faculty development policies. All of these concerns might well be summarized as faculty personnel management. Certainly the faculty input is a major resource of a university, and all aspects of this resource deserve careful and continuing attention.

The structural problem of a university is whether to handle faculty personnel management on a university-wide basis or on some intermediate basis. In some universities it is not unusual to have a dean of faculties as a part of the central administration who handles most details involved in coordinating departmental faculty actions. In some universities there are component faculties, as in arts and sciences, education, medicine, law, and other areas. The structural arrangement in any particular instance may be a matter of historical practice, the inclination of academic leaders, a consequence of size, or some other determinant.

I am not so much concerned here with structural arrangements as I am with functional differentiation. In many universities there is no clear-cut distinction between instructional matters and faculty personnel management. This is unfortunate, and it is one reason why performance and communication are often confused. Thus, it is not unusual to find in a university a college of arts and sciences and a faculty of arts and sciences with a single dean. What is not clearly understood is that such a structural arrangement combines two functions, the function of supervising a baccalaureate instructional program in arts and sciences and the function of supervising faculty personnel matters which embrace not alone the staffing of a baccalaureate program but also the staffing of a graduate program, research activities, re-education activities, consulting services, and other purposes of the university.

Let me make clear that I have no desire here to criticize any particular structural arrangement in a university. I do desire to criticize the failure to understand the functional distinction between supervision and coordination of an instructional program and the management of the faculty personnel resources of the university. To be sure, the two functions are closely related, but the two functions are also distinct. Thus, I would insist that supervision of departments on instruction of the undergraduate curriculum is different from supervision of departments on management of faculty personnel resources. As I have pointed out, the second embraces instructional and other activities of the university beyond the undergraduate program itself.

Let us turn now to the management function in general in a university. One of the academic myths of our time is that a university could operate just as well or perhaps better if there were no central administration, or if central administration were provided by a faculty committee. I realize that this statement is something of an exaggeration, and yet there are occasions when faculty criticism of central administration seems almost to be suggesting this position.

Before we consider the role of central administration in a university, we should acknowledge the fact that there are other basic operating units in a university besides academic departments. There may be a department of residence halls, one or more departments of student affairs and student health, a department of a university conference center, a department of a student activity center, and a department of intercollegiate athletics. There may be certain research institutes which exist outside the academic departments. And there will be a whole array of service and management departments essential to the operation of the university, such as buildings and grounds, purchasing and storage of supplies, maintenance of equipment, the collection of charges, and accounting. No university can be simply an aggregation of academic departments without these other accoutrements of an on-going enterprise. The scope of central administration in a university reaches beyond so-called academic affairs in its narrow sense.

Essentially, the role of central administration in a university is two-fold. It must manage the use of scarce input resources needed by the university enterprise, especially the input resources of current operating funds and of capital plant. Secondly, central administration must provide the leadership and top-direction in planning and programming the objectives and activities of the university. Management requires the augmentation and allocation of financial resources, the recruitment and retention of personnel, the provision of services such as supplies and telephones and the operation of plant. Top-direction involves questions of defining purposes, organizing to accomplish objectives, coordination of effort, evaluation of performance, reporting of accomplishments and problems, and internal communication. These are sizable assignments indeed, and they require top talent and dedicated effort.

Central administration may undertake directly much of the coordination of activity within a university, or as I have suggested some of the coordination and even some of the general management tasks may be delegated to a structure of coordination within the university. Again,

I am not advocating any particular structure but pleading for careful definition of the particular organizational arrangements which are utilized within a university.

In many instances today much of the coordination activity of a university is performed by the central administration. This is a desirable arrangement under two circumstances: when the coordination assignment can be performed by a small staff, and when the coordination burden is not heavy. In many instances, for example, the specialized research institutes may be coordinated on a university-wide basis. Continuing education activities are often coordinated on a university-wide basis. Public service activities are frequently coordinated on a university-wide basis. And, of course, faculty personnel management as well as well as coordination of instructional programs require some attention from central administration. The planning and programming of capital plant improvements will ordinarily be undertaken by central administration. To be sure, in a university various consultative devices may well exist in conjunction with all of these activities.

With this last observation, it is time to give more specific attention to communication as such, to the realization of a shared understanding of a shared purpose within a university. I have dealt at length upon matters of structure within a university because structure invariably complicates or conditions communication. This circumstance arises from several factors. One of them is again the unique characteristic of a university as an organized enterprise. Whereas entrepreneurial talent is a recognized input in a business and industrial enterprise, faculty talent is the nearest comparable input for a university. Management talent, as I have noted earlier, is an important ingredient of a university, but it is not quite the same as the entrepreneurial talent of business which combines ideas with management. In a university, management must develop ideas for the university as an organization, but it is the faculty which contributes the ideas for instruction and research.

The academic departments are more than basic operating units of a university. They are the major educational resource of the university. Colleges are more than structures of coordination for the academic departments. They are agencies of educational planning and development. The faculty or faculties of a university are more than an instrument of personnel management. They are the very technological process of higher education. The peculiar status of faculty members as parts of an academic department, of colleges, and of faculties is such that these individuals cannot be passive recipients of management communication. Faculty members are themselves a vital part of the entire university communications network.

The first problem of communications in a university is how to promote a sense of shared purpose. It has even been suggested that it is no longer realistic to speak of a shared purpose or of a university. Instead, we have been advised to use a new label, the "multiversity." The temptation to accept the suggestion is quite substantial. Yet, the university remains as an organizational entity, as a unit of enterprise in the social institution of higher education. A university may indeed have multiple types or kinds of output. A university is nonetheless a single agency of higher education. A university shares a reality of existence with all its constituent parts: faculty, students, alumni, administrators, staff, and others. It is this reality of existence, if nothing else, which provides every university with a shared purpose.

It is to me a shocking matter that so many participants in a university—faculty members, students, alumni, and sometimes others—often know so little about the financing of the enterprise. They are unaware of the relative role of charges, philanthropy, government, and borrowing in providing the current operating income and the capital plant resources of the university. They are even more unaware of the procedures and the social constraints involved in trying to augment any of these sources of income in order that operating expenditures may be increased and new or improved physical facilities may be provided. Too often the attitude seems to prevail that administrators should find the income and others should share in its expenditure. In a shared purpose, income and expenditure go hand in hand.

In the various instructional programs of the university, there is also a shared purpose. The degree received by the graduated student is awarded in the name of the university. The student and the alumnus associates himself with the university as well as with a particular college and a particular academic department. To some extent most students in a university will have instructional experience with more than one department, even with more than one college. The reputation of a university may rest upon some kind of evaluation of particular departments, but still it is the university as a whole which enjoys some common rating among the publics interested in higher education.

The research record of a few individuals in a university enlarges the research opportunity for a large number of persons in that university. The reputation of the student body, even if it be the reputation of only a small but highly articulate and visible part of the student body, will attach itself to the university as a unit. The instructional procedures and instructional effectiveness of particular faculty members become characteristic of the university as a whole.

It seems to me that more needs to be done in a university to arrive at communication of a shared purpose. Such communication will not be achieved by occasional public ceremonies, by newsletters and bulletins, and by fancy publications. All of these are important and have their appropriate place. But communication is much more; it is primarily a matter of continuing participation in the review and evaluation of academic activity and conditions. Communication must actively involve all members of a faculty and today must reach student leaders as well. Communication must concern problems and action, must look to improvements and new accomplishments, must seek the general will and individual achievement.

Communication must set as its goal not just a shared purpose but also shared understanding. The two are closely related. Indeed, I do not see how there can be a shared purpose in a university without a shared understanding. When a university does develop a sense of shared purpose, it will also probably have found a shared understanding.

One of the troubles of a university is a tendency for learning to be critical in tone. After all, much of knowledge involves not just blind acceptance of an existing stock of data and theory but a continuing reexamination of these. In matters of literary and artistic evaluation, standards of criticisms are the very essence of learning. In the consideration of social institutions and behavior, there is a general disposition to emphasize problems and deficiencies. The result is that higher education as a process and a university as an enterprise are often considered by many as engaged primarily in social and individual criticism. Sometimes this criticism is confused with subversion.

The learning to be critical needs always to be balanced by the wisdom of practical experience and action. It is simpler to criticize a play than to write one. It is simpler to criticize the conventional wisdom of economics than to propound a more realistic economic theory. It is simpler to criticize family failures than to set forth guide lines for family love and responsibility. It is simpler to criticize the voters than to get elected as a representative of the people.

Higher education is both science and art. As science, higher education is concerned with the state of current knowledge and practice in various fields and seeks to advance knowledge and practice. But as an art higher education is concerned with behavior and performance; it seeks first change in students themselves and then it seeks through individual action on a larger stage to promote new achievements in products and people. Higher education needs the learning to be critical but also the wisdom to perform effectively.

A shared understanding of higher education might well hope for two results: learning and wisdom about the university itself and then learning and wisdom about the world of which the university is but a part. Any lesser goal of the communications network will fall far short of the fundamental needs of our day.

The structure of a university may facilitate or hamper communication. I believe structure hampers communication when it is not clearly related to the technological process of higher education and to the desired outputs of higher education. I believe structure hampers communication also when it is not clearly defined in terms of function to be performed by the differentiated parts of the enterprise. Structure can facilitate communication when it is clearly related to the technology and outputs of higher education, and when it is clearly defined.

But structure is not a substitute for communication,

and it is no guarantee of communication. Communication requires participation of all elements of the academic community. Communication requires listeners as well as speakers, readers as well as writers, messages as well as media. Communication requires knowledge, interest, and commitment. Communication requires leadership. Communication requires the prospect of action. To put all these ingredients of communication together is a high art, worthy of the supreme artist.

Analogies, we all know, are dangerous. Yet we all indulge in them as a means of reinforcing our special and technical jargon. I like to think of organizational structure in an enterprise as the skeleton of the human body. I like to think of communication as the nervous system and the blood stream of the body. The skeleton is a structure of differentiated parts, but it is useless unless incorporated in a living, acting organism which is the human being himself. And the human being has a most amazing communications network, an information retrieval and processing unit, and an action system of blood, glandular secretions, and muscles. When we think of ourselves as individuals, we can appreciate some of the complexities of structure and communication in an enterprise like a university.

A university is a complicated organism. It is not easy to define its differentiated parts. It is not easy to establish its communications network, to operate its information retrieval and processing unit, to stimulate and execute action. Indeed, there is a widespread impression that a university as an enterprise is an especially slow-moving entity, somewhat rigid and set in its ways as to technology, reluctant to undertake innovation, occasionally careless as to its outputs, lacking in effective communication. To some extent, in varying ways in different universities, these impressions may be justified.

The major test of any university, it seems to me, is the effectiveness of its system of communication. Does there exist in a particular university a shared understanding of a shared purpose? If the answer is yes, or if the answer is more affirmative than negative, then I believe we may say about a university that it is achieving communication as part of a dynamic, continuing operation. But communication is never ended until an enterprise itself ceases to exist, until life itself is terminated.

Communication is life, endeavor, quest. No university has any reality without it. Communication is a pearl of creation, an act of artistry, a product of skill. No university can perform its mission without it. Communication is prelude to action, guide post to perfectability. Without it, no university is a university in its service to civilization.